SPEECH SYNTHESIS AND RECOGNITION SYSTEMS

ELLIS HORWOOD BOOKS IN COMPUTING SCIENCE

General Editors: Professor JOHN CAMPBELL, University College London, and BRIAN L. MEEK, King's College London (KQC), University of London

Series in Computers and Their Applications

Series Editor: BRIAN L. MEEK, Computer Centre, King's College London (KQC), University of London

Series continued at end of book

SPEECH SYNTHESIS AND RECOGNITION SYSTEMS

E. J. YANNAKOUDAKIS, B.Sc., Ph.D., FBCS, MIDPM
Department of Computer Science
University of Bradford
and
P. J. HUTTON, B.Sc., M.Sc.
Department of Computer Science
University of Bradford

ELLIS HORWOOD LIMITED
Publishers · Chichester

Halsted Press: a division of
JOHN WILEY & SONS
New York · Chichester · Brisbane · Toronto

First published in 1987 by
ELLIS HORWOOD LIMITED
Market Cross House, Cooper Street,
Chichester, West Sussex, PO19 1EB, England
The publisher's colophon is reproduced from James Gillison's drawing of the ancient Market Cross, Chichester.

Distributors:

Australia and New Zealand:
JACARANDA WILEY LIMITED
GPO Box 859, Brisbane, Queensland 4001, Australia

Canada:
JOHN WILEY & SONS CANADA LIMITED
22 Worcester Road, Rexdale, Ontario, Canada

Europe and Africa:
JOHN WILEY & SONS LIMITED
Baffins Lane, Chichester, West Sussex, England

North and South America and the rest of the world:
Halsted Press: a division of
JOHN WILEY & SONS
605 Third Avenue, New York, NY 10158, USA

© 1987 E.J. Yannakoudakis and P.J. Hutton/Ellis Horwood Limited

British Library Cataloguing in Publication Data
Yannakoudakis, E.J.
Speech synthesis and recognition systems. —
(Ellis Horwood series in computers and their applications).
1. Speech synthesis
I. Title   II. Hutton P.J.
006.5'4   TK7882.S65

Library of Congress Card No. 87–19832

ISBN 0–7458–0314–8 (Ellis Horwood Limited)
ISBN 0–470–20959–3 (Halsted Press)

Phototypeset in Times by Ellis Horwood Limited
Printed in Great Britain by R. J. Acford, Chichester

Contents

Preface

Speech synthesis and recognition, often called voice input and output (I/O), occupies a privileged place within the realm of man-machine communication. Voice I/O has received a great deal of attention during the last five years. It was after the public at large started using microcomputers that the subject of 'user-friendly' interfaces for man-machine communication became vital to the design of any type of computer system.

Other well-established media of communication with the computer are the keyboard, touch-sensitive screen, the mouse, the joystick, image processing devices, etc. Because language is the most natural means of communication, speech synthesis and recognition systems are by far the most desirable means for communicating with the computer, but they are, at the same time, very difficult to computerise effectively.

When the sound spectrograph was invented approximately forty years ago, phoneticians and linguists were confident that the mysteries of voice would be solved and the inherent characteristics of speech would at last be understood. Unfortunately this has not happened, for a number of reasons: (a) inadequate computer architectures, especially their slow speed, (b) noise and interference, which are very difficult to deal with while communicating with the computer, (c) accents of individuals and the characteristics of their vocal tracts, (d) the unpredictable manner in which words and sentences are formed.

Although the market currently offers a number of voice I/O kits for converting text to audible speech or recognising spoken words, these operate rather mechanically and have limited vocabularies. Voice-processing tools, generally, give little insight into the spoken word. We still cannot answer questions like 'is there a common voice pattern between different speakers?' 'Is there a universal set of phonemes which govern human voice production?' 'Is there any relationship between human speech and other natural sounds?' 'Can we create a stochastic model of speech?' If we can provide answers to some of these fundamental questions, we can then begin to gain insight into human speech and phonetics. A major aim of this book has been to discuss the human physiology and how it affects speech production in general.

Before human speech can be processed by the computer, it must first be digitised so that it can be stored on a computer-readable medium for further processing. The higher the rate at which speech signals are digitised, the better the quality of speech will be; the rate is measured in kilobits per second. Digitisation is accomplished by a voice coder which aims to encode and reproduce sound waveform signals that are acceptable to the human ear as natural speech.

There are two basic approaches to encoding, namely, waveform and parametric coding. A waveform coder usually operates at a speed of over 6.0 kilobits per second and can also be used to encode signals other than speech. A parametric coder ('vocoder') usually operates at speeds less than 6.0 kilobits per second and the techniques employed attempt to approximate the speech signals on the basis of a reference model for speech production. Note that the lower the speed, the more complicated the coder becomes in order to achieve satisfactory speech reproduction. Also, the lower the speed, the less natural the 'voice' then sounds, but of course the costs of system design (e.g. fewer logic gates/circuits), transmission and storage drop.

There is a paradox here regarding the hardware under discussion. Although the variables and parameters (e.g. speed, complexity) are basically quantifiable, it becomes very difficult to establish the precise cross-over points between synthetic communications and high-quality speech reproduction. The current crossing point between a vocoder and a waveform coder lies approximately between 6.8 and 8.5 kilobits per second.

In this book we introduce the technology of speech synthesis and recognition, starting with the phonetic aspects of the human language and the problems which hinder its full implementation and intelligent manipulation by the computer. Next, we present the most well known techniques for digital coding of speech and their capabilities. The functional components of voice I/O systems are then presented from the conceptual point of view, that is, without reference to existing systems and devices already available in the market. Finally, we describe two typical speech-processing languages and the facilities they offer the general user for voice synthesis and recognition.

We also include in an Appendix a complete program, written in Pascal, to convert text to phonemes by following a set of rules. The latter are read by the program from a separate file. The structure of the program makes it independent of the actual rules used, enabling the extension of the rules, their refinement, and updating when necessary. Apart from its obvious use as a piece of software to generate phonemes from free-running text, it can also be modified to generate the actual parameters for a speech synthesiser. Moreover, the program can be extended to produce phonological statistics on the written language, which can then be utilised by an intelligent voice-processing system (e.g. to reconstruct mutilated messages using a probabilistic model).

Because of the interdisciplinary nature of research efforts on voice I/O systems, encompassing areas such as linguistics, phonetics, syntactics, electronic engineering, communications engineering and of course computer science, the researcher (let alone the student) finds it very difficult to acquire fundamental knowledge and to become familiar with the required terminology. We believe that the Glossary included will help the reader to understand the basic terminology of speech synthesis and recognition systems.

We believe that the book will be useful to all people interested in speech synthesis and recognition systems, since it offers an introduction to the basic techniques of storing and processing speech signals. Because the material does not require any *a priori* knowledge of the subject, we believe that the book will be useful both, to undergraduate students taking courses in man-machine interfaces and artificial intelligence, and to postgraduate students researching the area of man-machine interfaces.

Acknowledgements

We should like to express our gratitude to Mr Duncan Stickings (Computer Officer at the University of Bradford) for his invaluable comments and suggestions regarding the implementation of the program for text-to-phoneme decomposition.

We are also indebted to Mr Glenn Hutton for his help regarding the presentation of the material.

We are most grateful to Voice Systems International (Cambridge, UK) for permission to use material from the manuals describing the Voice Processing Language (V.P.L.) of VOTAN, and the text-to-speech language of INFOVOX.

1

Speech

1.1 INTRODUCTION

Speech is the most natural means of communication and provides the means to communicate our thoughts and pass information. The sucessful computerisation of the speech process has, however, eluded computer scientists and linguists for more than forty years. Governments and private industry have spent millions of pounds trying to produce machines which can both listen to and produce speech.

Speech synthesis and recognition pose their own problems (Yannakoudakis, 1985) and in order to understand these it is necessary to have some knowledge of the speech process.

In this chapter, we are going to discuss some aspects of acoustics for the benefit of the non-specialist (Ladefoged, 1966), as well as the effect that human physiology has upon the production of speech, by considering the characteristics of the various articulatory organs of humans. We also discuss how human physiology effects speech processing by the computer.

1.2 SPEECH PROCESS

Speech consists of a continuously varying sound wave which links speaker to listener. Sound requires a medium through which to travel and the most usual medium is air, though other media such as water, wood, glass, etc., are suitable.

When we make a sound, we disturb the molecules of air nearest to our mouths, these molecules being disturbed in a manner which sets them oscillating about their point of rest. Each molecule will propagate this effect as it collides with other molecules in its near vicinity and a chain reaction will begin. This reaction will eventually dissipate some distance from the speaker. The distance travelled depends on the energy initially imparted by the vocal organs.

As previously mentioned, a sound wave is caused by the vibration of a molecule. If that molecule is given a hard 'knock' then it will move further from its point of rest than if it had received a light one. The maximum distance it moves from its point of origin (point of rest), is known as the 'amplitude' of vibration. One complete cycle starts from its point of rest, goes to the maximum displacement at one side, then the other side, and finally returns again to its point of rest. The number of times this complete cycle occurs in one second is known as the 'frequency'.

The time it takes to complete a cycle varies, irrespective of amplitude, and is referred to as the cycle 'period'; one cycle is otherwise known as one hertz. Obviously, some cycles take longer to complete than others. Fig. 1.1

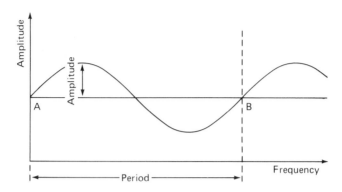

Fig. 1.1 — A periodic sound wave.

shows a complete cycle from point A to point B, represented as a sine wave. Sounds which possess the same 'period' for successive cycles are known as 'periodic sounds', whereas those that do not are known as 'aperiodic' sounds. Fig. 1.1 shows a periodic sound wave.

An example of a periodic sound is the note produced by striking a tuning fork, where the sound stays fairly constant until it dies away. Periodic sounds give rise to a clear perception of pitch, such that the higher the frequency the higher the pitch.

Not all periodic sounds are as simple as the above illustration may suggest. The 'shape' of the sound wave can be influenced by the presence of what are known as 'harmonics'. A harmonic is a sound wave whose frequency is a simple multiple of the fundamental frequency. The fundamental frequency is in fact the lowest harmonic. Thus if f represents the fundamental frequency, harmonics with the frequency, $2f$, $3f$, $4f$, $5f$, etc., can be obtained.

The more harmonics there are in the sound wave, the more complex the curve becomes, moving away from the simple sinusoidal shape. Fig. 1.2(c) shows a more complex wave than the one presented in Fig. 1.1. In fact, the wave in Fig. 1.2(c) is the combination of the harmonics in Figs 1.2(a) and 1.2(b). We frequently decompose complex sine waves into their constituent harmonics using mathematical formulae known as 'Fourier series', so that we can then process these further.

Aperiodic sounds are those whose pattern does not repeat itself as in the case of a periodic sound. An aperiodic sound can be represented by a spectrum, which is in the form of a continuous line indicating the amplitude

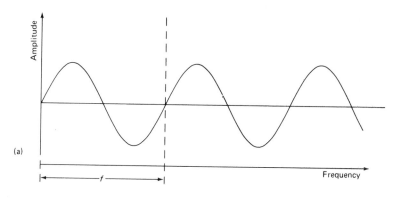

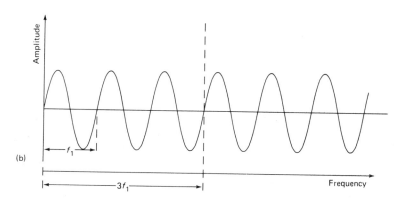

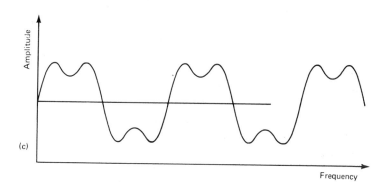

Fig. 1.2 — (a) and (b) sine waves where f is the fundamental frequency; (c) a non-sinusoidal but periodic sound wave composed from two sound waves.

of vibration at every frequency (there is no fundamental frequency and consequently there are no harmonics). Fig. 1.3 shows the form of an aperiodic sound.

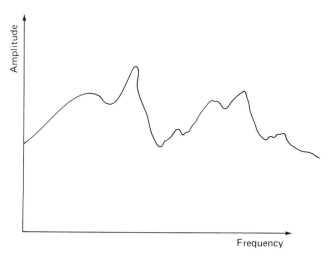

Fig. 1.3 — An aperiodic sound wave.

Two sounds, with the same fundamental frequency, can sound different, so the same note obtained from different musical instruments does not sound the same; both the quality and sound differ, even though the note is the same. These diversities occur because of the differences in the harmonics, certain harmonics having been attenuated or amplified depending on the instrument concerned.

Note that sound can be increased in amplitude by its transmission from one medium to another. For example, in a guitar the bridge transmits the vibrations made by the strings to the wooden body, with noticeable increase in amplitude; the guitar body acts as a resonator.

The transmission of vibrations from one medium to another is referred to as 'resonance' and the receiving body is referred to as the 'resonator'. We must note here that volumes of air can be set resonating, as well as solid mediums.

Every resonator has what is known as a 'natural resonant frequency'; that is, a frequency to which it will most readily respond. Some resonators only respond to frequencies close to their natural resonant frequency, while others will respond to a far wider range of frequencies. Consequently, if we input a sound wave consisting of a large number of frequencies (all with the same amplitude) into a resonating chamber, then there will be a significant difference in the output between the frequencies close to the resonant frequency and those furthest away. Those closest to the resonant frequency will be significantly increased, whilst those frequencies furthest away will be attenuated.

Let us use an example to illustrate the extent to which a resonator responds to different frequencies. Fig. 1.4 shows the difference between two resonating bodies, (a) and (b), both having a natural resonant frequency of 50 Hz. In other words, their maximum amplitude is reached by an input

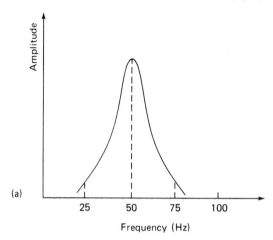

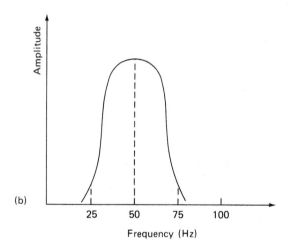

Fig. 1.4 — Examples of resonance curves.

vibration with a frequency of 50 cycles per second. However, the response of (a) drops more rapidly than the response of (b).

What we are saying is that the output from a resonating body is determined more by its own characteristics than by the input it receives. This is particularly relevant with human speech because of the inherent physiological differences between individuals.

1.3   THE HUMAN SPEECH PROCESS

The sounds produced by the vocal cords of man are rather weak but have a wide range of frequencies. The vocal cords provide the fundamental frequencies which are then utilised by the three resonating chambers (a) the oral cavity, (b) the nasal cavity and (c) the pharynx.

In addition, when we speak we use a combination of the following:

(1)   Larynx (vibration source)
(2)   Lungs (energy source)
(3)   Vocal tract (resonance source)
(4)   Nasal cavity (resonance source)
(5)   Articulatory organs (to change the 'shape' of the resonant cavities).

By altering the movements of the various speech organs, man is capable of producing a wide variety of sounds, where each organ plays its own part in speech production.

1.3.1 The larynx

The larynx, better known as the 'voice box', is situated just behind the adam's apple. It contains two folds of skin, known as the vocal cords, which vibrate to produce sound and are the primary source of voice production.

The vibration of the vocal cords depends on their mass. The greater the mass, the fewer the vibrations per second; or, conversely, the lower the mass the faster the cords vibrate.

The frequency with which the vocal cords vibrate determines the pitch of the voice. High-pitched sounds are high-frequency sounds, as found in women and children. Their high-pitched voices are a result of the mass of the vocal cords being low, consequently allowing a high number of vibrations per second. In a male the typical range is 50 to 250 Hz, whereas in a female the range can go up to approximately 500 Hz.

Speech sounds are produced either with the vocal cords vibrating, such as with all English vowels, or without the vibration of the vocal cords. The process of using voiced sounds, with the vocal cords vibrating, is called 'phonation'. Sounds produced without the vibration of the vocal cords are known as voiceless sounds, as is the case for /p/, /t/ and /k/ (slashes denote sounds).

Another important feature here is the 'glottis,' which is the term used for the space between the vocal cords. The glottis can be used to block the flow of air. The result is that pressure builds up beneath the glottis from the lungs, which is then released explosively, creating what is known as a 'glottal stop'. Examples of this can be heard in various regional accents, although strictly speaking the English language does not have any glottal sounds. The following sentence illustrates this (the glottal stops are represented by an apostrophe):

PU' A BE'ER BI' O BU'ER ON YOUR KNIFE

(PUT A BETTER BIT OF BUTTER ON YOUR KNIFE)

1.3.2 The lungs

The physiology of the human respiratory system (see Fig. 1.5) provides the required energy to set the vocal cords into motion. As man inhales air, the lungs expand and so does the thoracic cavity.

The exhalation of air from the lungs forces air past the larynx, this energy source being utilised to set the vocal cords vibrating. Additionally, the passage of air can be obstructed, enabling the production of certain speech sounds. The degree of obstruction can vary, as for example in the sound /p/ or /b/ which requires a total obstruction, whereas the sound /f/ requires only partial obstruction and is known as a 'fricative consonant'.

The lungs are also responsible for the amplitude of sound, that is, how loud the receiver perceives the sound. This depends on the energy with which the air is forced past the vocal cords. The more energy provided the greater will be the displacement of the vocal cords. Thus, the greater the displacement the greater will be the amplitude of the resulting sound wave.

1.3.3 The vocal tract

The air passages above the vocal cords are known collectively as the vocal tract, which extends from the larynx to the lips and includes the oral cavity. The oral cavity, in particular, makes a large contribution to the overall sound production. This is due to the fact that it can vary in shape considerably, primarily as a result of the mobility of the tongue and jaws.

The vocal tract acts as a resonant cavity amplifying certain frequencies and attenuating others. The rate of vibration of the vocal cords determines the fundamental frequency, and the resonant frequencies are determined by the shape of the vocal tract at any given instant, plus the accompanying fundamental frequency.

During the process of speech, the tongue and lips are in continuous motion, resulting in a constantly changing shape and size in the vocal tract. In consequence, this creates changes in the resonant frequency, which in turn alter the accompanying harmonics. This implies that speech consists of a continuously varying sound wave.

The vocal tract is also responsible for the production of peaks in the energy spectrum of the speech wave. These peaks are called 'formants'. They arise when the position of the articulatory organs remains static, as a result of which the vocal tract resonates at three or four overtone frequencies. However, formant resonances move during continuous speech owing to the change in the size and shape of the vocal tract, but the rate of change is relatively slow because of the physical limitations on just how quickly we can move our tongue, lips, jaw, etc.

Assuming a typical distance of 17 cm between the tongue and lips, and the speed of sound $c=340$ metres per second, then resonances are produced at 500 Hz, 1500 Hz and 2500 Hz. These formants are usually numbered as $F1$ (approximately 500 Hz), $F2$ (approximately 1780 Hz), $F3$ (approximately 2500 Hz), etc.

Although most vowels have more than three formants, the first three are

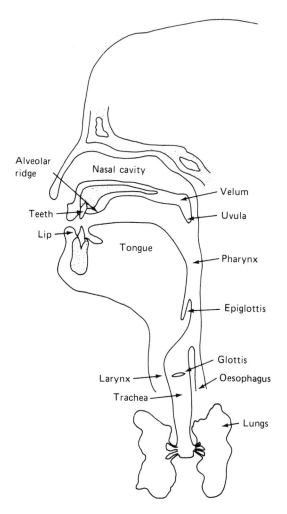

Fig. 1.5 — Anatomy of the human speech system.

sufficient to characterise and identify them (the rest are primarily concerned with the voice quality of the individual speaker).

The vocal tract size varies considerably from one speaker to another, as a result of which the formant frequencies become highly speaker-dependent. It is not only the vocal tract size which affects the formant frequencies but also the fundamental frequency, sound being produced, and the vocal tract shape as a whole.

The vocal tract acts as a source of consonant production as well as a resonator for vowels and consonants. Therefore, consonantal sounds may also exemplify a clear formant structure, as is the case with the consonants /l/, /m/ and /n/.

1.3.4   The nasal cavity

This is the cavity coupled to the oral tract by a passage at the back of the mouth, the passage being guarded by a flap of skin known as the 'velum'. With the aid of the velum, air is allowed to pass outside the body via the nose.

The nasal cavity introduces formant resonances similar to the vocal tract. Whereas it might be expected that these formants are fixed (as there is no means of significantly altering the size of the nasal cavity) this in fact is not the case. Both nasal and oral cavities operate in unison in the production of sound.

Speech sounds which are produced without the aid of the nasal cavity are known as 'non-nasal' sounds. Conversely, those produced with the passage of air through the nasal cavity are known as 'nasal' sounds. An example of a nasal sound is /n/, whereas /r/ is a non-nasal sound. These sounds are highlighted when a person suffers from a cold; the nasal cavity is affected because the passage of air is limited or blocked, and speech production is significantly altered.

1.3.5   The articulatory organs

The production of different sounds uses a combination of the following articulatory organs.

The lips
The formation of various lip shapes facilitates in the production of vowels and various consonants, such as /p/ and /b/.

The teeth
The teeth are used in conjunction with the lips to produce sounds, such as /v/ and /f/.

The alveolar ridge
This ridge forms the point of contact with the tip of the tongue and is used in the production of sounds, such as /t/, /d/ and /n/.

The tongue
This muscular organ is very agile and the point of contact of the tongue with various parts of the mouth gives rise to many distinctive sounds.

The jaws
The movement of the jaws alters the size and shape of the oral cavity.

The cheeks
A build-up of pressure in the oral cavity is facilitated by the cheeks. This pressure is necessary for the correct pronunciation of certain sounds, such as /p/ and /b/.

1.4 PROBLEMS ASSOCIATED WITH THE HUMAN SPEECH PROCESS

As mentioned previously, the frequency with which the vocal cords vibrate is dependent on the mass of the cords. This mass varies from speaker to speaker and, in consequence, the fundamental frequency will also vary from speaker to speaker. Because the harmonics also depend on the fundamental frequency these too will be different.

In addition, the resonating chambers in the vocal tract vary between individuals, and according to the position of articulatory organs this variation, in turn, leads to variations in the manner harmonics are amplified and attenuated. All these variations lead to different sound waves being emitted from individuals producing the same word.

It has been demonstrated that we tend to make guesses on the basis of what we expect to hear (Cole, 1973). In tests carried out it has been shown that poorly pronounced words when spoken in isolation have a low recognition rate, but when the same words are spoken in context (Tulving and Gold, 1963; Morton, 1964) then the recognition rate increases. This feature can be attributed to the ability man has to cluster and associate words by concept and therefore place a higher probability of occurrence to these words that are clustered under the concept (topic) in discussion. The linguistic redundancy (i.e. information that can be postulated by knowing the syntactic and grammatical rules of a language, as well as the semantics) present in most languages also helps improve recognition.

Acoustic analysis of speech has shown that there is an abundance of acoustic information produced during the speech process. However, man is unable to perceive all this information; for example, the same word said in apparently identical manner by the same person, when analysed acoustically, will produce differing results. Conversely, when we hear sounds we perceive them to be identical, and more importantly we perceive words spoken by different speakers to be the same even though there may be significant differences in pitch, intonation, stress, etc.

The above considerations suggest that as humans we are either incapable of perceiving all the acoustic information present, or if we are capable then we are not aware of the levels required to identify sounds. Just how much information we are able to perceive is a question that still remains unanswered. We know for example, that the lower two formants (i.e. $F1$ and $F2$) can be used to distinguish one vowel sound from another, whereas the upper two formants apparently tell us something about the quality of an individual's voice. However, we still do not know how we 'normalise' across different speakers to enable us to recognise acoustically different words as being the same.

One way of determing what is necessary for identifying different sounds is by filtering out certain frequencies and ascertaining whether or not the results are acceptable to the human ear. We are here referring to synthetic speech, which is also useful from this perspective since its acoustics are generally much simpler than normal speech.

1.5   THE EAR

Generally speaking, speech synthesis systems are as good as the human ear judges them to be. Individual elements (e.g. words, sentences) must be clearly identifiable, easy to interpret (phonetically) and subsequently pass over to the brain for semantic processing.

There is much to be learned from studying the process through which humans decode the incoming speech signal (Delgutte, 1984). We know that the human brain receives the signal after it has passed through the peripheral auditory system. It has been demonstrated that there is a difference between the incoming signal and that received at the eighth cranial nerve. Unfortunately, little is known about the process beyond this point.

In the next section, we are going to discuss briefly the physiological characteristics of the ear and the way it filters and distorts the incoming sound waves.

1.5.1   The external ear

This consists of what we normally think of as 'the ear', together with a channel leading to the ear-drum. The channel is filled with air, and can itself act as a resonator, causing some amplification of frequencies near its resonant frequency. This in fact leads to some distortion of the original sounds produced.

Sound waves are passed down the channel to the ear-drum, with the vibrations of the sound waves causing the ear-drum to vibrate. However, there are limitations to the frequencies at which the ear-drum can vibrate, and not all the frequencies present in the sound waves cause vibrations. The upper limit of frequencies is put at about 20 000 Hz, although in older people this may be considerably reduced. The ear-drum therefore acts as a filter for some of the frequencies received, although not all people respond to the same range of frequencies.

1.5.2   The middle ear

The middle ear lies behind the ear-drum and is a small air-filled cavity which contains the three auditory ossicles or bonelets (see Fig. 1.6). These are the 'anvil', 'stirrup' and 'hammer', appropriately named because of their resemblance to these objects. The hammer is attached to the ear-drum, the anvil is attached to the inner end of the hammer and, on the other side, to the stirrup. The bottom of the stirrup is fastened into an opening in the side of the brain case through which it comes into contact with the mechanism of the internal ear discussed below. The purpose of these little bones is to pick up sound waves caught by the ear-drum, amplify them and then transmit these to the internal ear.

The middle ear does not transfer all frequencies equally. It operates at its best at around 2000 Hz, with efficiency falling off at high and low frequencies. In other words, it also acts as a filter and it amplifies/attenuates certain frequencies, leading to further distortion of the incoming sound waves.

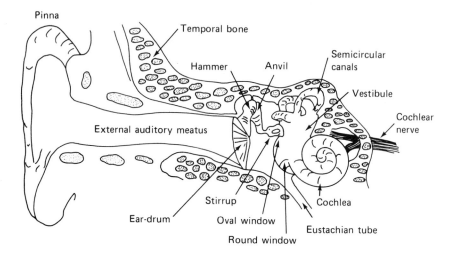

Fig. 1.6 — Anatomy of the human ear.

1.5.3 The internal ear
The physiological features of the human ear we have discussed so far are only accessories for sound reception. The real sense organ, that is, the fundamental ear structure, lies deeper still.

The internal ear is buried inside the framework of the brain case, with the bottom of the stirrup lying in a small opening of the brain case. This opening leads directly to a liquid-filled space known as the 'cochlea', which is a long structure coiled like a snail shell with two and a half turns (which when unrolled measures appoximately 35 mm).

The internal ear is filled with fluid and is partitioned along most of its length into two separate channels. There are two openings of the inner ear into the middle ear, one for each side of the partition. The stirrup is connected to one opening, known as the 'oval window'. The other opening is covered by an elastic membrane which facilitates changes in the pressure of the fluid. This second opening is known as the 'round window'.

When the stirrup transfers its vibrations to the fluid, which in turn vibrates, the dividing membrane or partition also takes up some of the vibration. However, because of its structure, it responds to different vibration frequencies at different positions along its length. This information (the frequencies recieved) is then passed to the brain for further processing, about which we know very little.

As a result of the various mechanisms within the ear through which sound waves pass, the sound eventually received by the brain has been slightly amplified or attenuated and certain frequencies filtered. Hence, sound perceived by different individuals varies as a direct result of physical differences in the structure of the hearing mechanism.

2
Phonetic aspects of language and problem areas

2.1 INTRODUCTION

It is well known that written words are not always related to their phonetic counterparts, and this in effect makes it rather difficult for a learner to master the orthography of a language. It is also true that some languages are better than others in this respect. For example, in Greek, individual letters that occur in a word are usually pronounced, with the exception of a few combinations of vowels, such as EI and OI which produce a single phoneme. In English, however, it becomes more dificult to master the orthography because a substantial number of letters in words remain silent, as for example in the words DAUGHTER, COLONEL and KNIFE.

In this chapter we introduce the phonetic aspects of human language (O'Connor, 1984; Singh and Singh, 1976) and consider the problems which hinder its full use and intelligent manipulation by speech synthesis systems. We must point out here that our discussion is centred around the English language, although in many cases our considerations are equally applicable to most Western languages.

2.2 PHONETIC TRANSCRIPTION

2.2.1 The phone

The sounds of speech are rarely heard by themselves but within the context of words. The individual sounds of speech are known as phones, which are the minimum unit of identifiable speech. These are distinct sounds which we can recognise.

When we speak we are often unaware of the differences between certain phones. For example, there are three perceptually different 'p' phones in the words 'pit', 'pat' and 'put'. These differences arise because when we are articulating the 'p' sound in the words, we are anticipating the position required by our articulatory organs for the next phone (i.e. the differing vowel sounds following the 'p' cause the variations in articulation).

Our articulatory organs cannot jump from one target position to the next discretely, but perform a blending process on the target positions, giving rise to a smooth but continuous flow. Thus, for 'p' there can be as many variations as there are following vowel sounds. Often we are not aware of these differences whilst speaking. The notion of differing sounds being considered similar leads us onto the phonetic concept of the phoneme.

2.2.2 The phoneme

Speech sounds (phones) can be represented by phonemes. A phoneme can be thought of as an organisational convenience, which brings relative simplicity out of a great complexity of sounds, rather than representing an actual sound as in the case of a phone. For example all the different [p] allophones in the words 'pit', 'pat' and 'put' would be grouped together under the /p/ phoneme. Square brackets are used to signify that it is an actual sound whereas slashes are used to signify a logical unit. The criteria for allocating different phones to a phoneme are not necessarily based on logic alone but also on what 'sounds right' within the context.

In essence, the rules for allocating phones to phonemes are:

(a) The phones are perceived to be the same by the speaker and therefore the same phoneme is allocated to each phone.

(b) A group of phones which have been placed together to make the phoneme are known as 'allophones'. Generally, allophones have a 'complementary distribution', that is, they cannot replace one another. The phoneme often corresponds to our concept of segmentation (i.e. the places in a word where, by changing a phoneme, the whole meaning of the word is changed).

The following example illustrates segmentation. In the word 'tin' the letters 't', 'i' and 'n' are phonemes corresponding to our notion of segmentation (i.e. by changing one phoneme the whole meaning of the word is changed), as in

tin, pin

tin, tan

tin, tip

Compare this now to the 'p' sounds in the words 'pin' and 'put' which are two allophones of the /p/ phoneme.

(c) A phoneme can be pronounced in slightly different ways. The way it is pronounced depends on both the following phone and, in some cases, the preceding one. This dependence is known as 'co-articulation' and it has been shown that the English language is mostly anticipatory. Thus, allophones differ in ways which can be predicted from the context in which they occur in that the differences often arise because of co-articulation.

Whereas an allophone can be substituted by another without changing its meaning, a phoneme cannot be substituted by another of its kind without losing its meaning. There are a few exceptions, notably [f] and [v], which are usually left as they are.

In conclusion, then, it can be said that an allophone aims to refine a phoneme by taking account of preceding and following sounds within specific contexts.

2.2.3   The International Phonetic Alphabet (I.P.A.)

An important aspect of phonetics is the accurate recording (writing down) of speech sounds as heard. To this end, an unambiguous means of representing speech sounds is required. There are several established systems for doing this, but one of the most widely used is the International Phonetic Alphabet (I.P.A.), which is presented in Fig. 2.1 (Bristow, 1984). It is worthy of mention at this point that the number of sounds transcribed depends on how narrow that transcription is. For example, the phoneme level would represent a broad transcription, whereas the allophone a narrow one.

The need for an I.P.A. has arisen because of the differences between the written form (orthography) and the spoken form. If the two were identical, we would have no need for phonetic transcriptions. The differences have arisen because once written down, a word can become 'frozen', whereas speech is constantly changing (although somewhat slowly).

The I.P.A. utilises a system of arbitrary symbols to represent speech sounds as used in all the languages of the world. The set of phonemes that a language requires can be regarded as the set of units needed to transcribe unambiguously the spoken word for that language. A language may use a subset of the I.P.A. speech sounds, as opposed to the full range of sounds available.

The I.P.A. adopts the following written distinctions between the phone and phoneme:

(a)   Allophones or phones are enclosed in square brackets (e.g. [p]) to signify that they are actual sounds.
(b)   Phonemes are placed between slashes (e.g. /l/) to signify that they are the logical units referred to rather than actual sounds.

The I.P.A. provides a large number of symbols for representing the different phonemes of a language, together with a number of diacritical markers. When these markers are used with the symbol for the phoneme they give additional information as to how that allophone is to be realised. Examples of diacritical symbols (usually appearing in superscripts) are: h for aspirated (i.e. a pronounced consonant followed immediately by a puff of breath), ~ for velarised (i.e. a sound produced with the back part of the tongue raised towards the velum) or pharyngealised (i.e. a consonant phonated at the pharynx), and ⊓ for dental articulation (i.e. consonant produced with the tip of the tongue touching the upper teeth).

The problem with systems such as the I.P.A. is that they are designed for the linguist and not for the computer scientist who aims to create models of analogue signals where precision and consistency are the guiding factors in the design process. Whereas linguists can afford to and do indeed approxi-

THE INTERNATIONAL PHONETIC ALPHABET

		Bilabial	Labiodental	Dental, Alveolar, or Post-alveolar	Retroflex	Palato-alveolar	Palatal
S O N A N T S (pulmonic air-stream mechanism)	Nasal	m	ɱ	n	ɳ		ɲ
	Plosive	p b		t d	ʈ ɖ		c ɟ
	(Median) Fricative	ɸ β	f v	θ ð s z	ʂ ʐ	ʃ ʒ	ç j
	(Median) Approximant		ʋ	ɹ	ɻ		j
	Lateral Fricative			ɬ ɮ			
	Lateral (Approximant)			l	ɭ		ʎ
	Trill			r			
	Tap or Flap			ɾ	ɽ		
C O N S (non-pulmonic air-stream)	Ejective	p'		t'			
	Implosive	ɓ		ɗ			
	(Median) Click	ʘ		ʇ ʗ			
	Lateral Click			ʖ			

DIACRITICS

- ₒ Voiceless ŋ̊ d̥
- . Voiced ş ţ
- ʰ Aspirated tʰ
- ͪ Breathy-voiced b̤ a̤
- ̪ Dental t̪
- ̫ Labialised t̫
- ̡ Palatalised t̡
- - Velarised or Pharyngealised t, ł
- ̩ Syllabic ņ ļ
- ͡ or ͜ Simultaneous sf (but see also under the heading Affricates)

- · or . Raised eˑ, ẹ, e̝ w
- · or ̩ Lowered eˑ, ẹ, e̞ ʁ
- ₊ Advanced u+, u̟
- - or ₋ Retracted i̠, i-, t̠
- ¨ Centralised ë
- ˜ Nasalised ã
- ˞, ˞, ʴ r-coloured aʴ
- : Long aː
- · Half-long aˑ
- ˘ Non-syllabic ŭ
- › More rounded ɔ›
- ‹ Less rounded y‹

OTHER SYMBOLS

- ɕ, ʑ Alveolo-palatal fricatives
- ʄ, ʒ̢ Palatalised ʃ, ʒ
- ɼ Alveolar fricative trill
- ɺ Alveolar lateral flap
- ɧ Simultaneous ʃ and x
- ʃˢ Variety of ʃ resembling s, etc.
- ɪ = ι
- ʊ = ɷ
- ɜ = Variety of ə
- ɚ = r-coloured ə

Fig. 2.1 — The International Phonetic alphabet (I.P.A.) (From G. Bristow: *Electronic Speech Synthesis*, Granada, 1984)

(Revised to 1979)

Velar		Uvular		Labial-Palatal	Labial-Velar		Pharyngeal		Glottal	
	ŋ		N							
k	g	q	ɢ		k͡p	g͡b			ʔ	
x	ɣ	χ	ʁ			ʍ	ħ	ʕ	h	ɦ
	ɰ			ɥ		w				
		R								
		ʀ								
k'										
	ɠ									

Front		Back	VOWELS	Front		Back	STRESS, TONE (PITCH)
i	ɨ	ɯ	Close	y	ʉ	u	' stress, placed at beginning of stressed syllable :
ɪ				ʏ		ɵ	, secondary stress : ¯ high level pitch, high tone :
e		ɤ	Half-close	ø		o	_ low level : ´ high rising :
	ə				ɵ		ˏ low rising : ` high falling :
ɛ		ʌ	Half-open	œ		ɔ	ˎ low falling : ˆ rise-fall :
æ	ɐ						ˇ fall-rise.
a		ɑ	Open	ɶ		ɒ	AFFRICATES can be written as digraphs, as ligatures, or with slur marks ; thus ts, tʃ, dʒ : ts̪ tʃ dʒ : t͡s t͡ʃ d͡ʒ. c, ɟ may occasionally be used for tʃ, dʒ.
Unrounded				Rounded			

Fig. 2.1 — The International Phonetic alphabet (I.P.A.) (From G. Bristow: *Electronic Speech Synthesis*, Granada, 1984)

mate sounds, computer scientists find it very difficult to implement systems which cannot be defined accurately. It is, therefore, not surprising that computer scientists are currently looking at alternative means of storing and manipulating 'imprecise' data (De Mori, 1983) and knowledge using 'expert systems' (De Mori, et al, 1987; Johnson *et al.*, 1985). The program we present in Appendix A can be characterised as an expert system for the decomposition of words into phonemes using a set of rules that have been derived empirically.

2.3 CLASSIFICATION SYSTEMS

A 'vowel' is a speech sound which is characterised by the lack of any closure or constriction in the vocal tract. Vowels are all voiced. Phonetically, vowels are a class of phonemes which occupy similar positions in words and other structures.

A 'consonant' is a speech sound opposite to the vowel; in other words, it is characterised by constriction or closure in the vocal tract. Consonants can be produced with or without voicing. Phonetically, consonants are also a class of phonemes occupying other positions marginal to the vowel position.

A 'diphthong' can be thought of as a sound which starts off as though it is aiming for the target position for one vowel, but ends up with the target position for another. A diphthong could be said to be a changing sound, as opposed to a static one. A good example of a diphthong is found in the word 'how'.

At school most of us are taught that there are 5 vowels (a, e, i, o, u) and 21 consonants. However, phonetically speaking, there are approximately 24 consonants and 19 vowel/diphthong phonemes. All 43 consonants and vowels/diphthongs, plus the co-articulation differences, are necessary to transcribe the English language accurately.

There are fundamental differences in the production of vowel sounds as opposed to consonant sounds. One of the most important differences lies in the fact that in consonant production there is some restriction to the flow of air from the lungs due to articulatory contact, or a narrowing of the vocal tract. This is not the case for vowels. Also, as mentioned previously, vowels are always voiced, whereas this is not the case for all consonants. It follows therefore that vowels and consonants have different classification systems.

The position of the vocal organs has proved to be of great help in the acoustic analysis of speech. Phoneticians have come up with many different ways of classifying phonemes into different groups on the basis of the positions/actions of the articulatory organs. A brief summary follows, examining these positions and phonetic classifications.

2.3.1 Vowel classification
Vowels tend to be articulated in a non-discrete manner, which can make them difficult to transcribe. The various vowel sounds can be classified according to (1) position of the tongue, (2) degree of muscle tenseness, (3) tongue tip curling and (4) degree of lip rounding.

2.3.1.1 *Position of the tongue*

Vowel production in the English language is achieved by positioning the tongue in three general locations within the oral cavity. These are accomplished by movement of the tongue along the horizontal axis, and is commonly referred to as tongue 'advancement'.

The nature and quality of the vowel produced is influenced by the shape of the individual oral cavity. In vowel production the position of the tongue is either to the front, central, or to the back of the mouth, thus altering the resonating cavity with different vowels.

Apart from the tongue's capability of assuming three positions along the horizontal axis, it can simultaneously move along the vertical axis. As a result, the tongue can assume a total of nine positions which represent the production of the eight English vowels. Table 2.1 presents some phonemes

Table 2.1 — Vowels distinguishable by the position of the tongue alone

Phoneme	I.P.A. transcription and example words				
/i/	as in	/it/ , 'eat'	/bit/ 'beet'	and	/bi/ 'bee'
/u/	as in	/uz/ , 'ooze'	/but/ 'boot'	and	/fu/ 'shoe'
/e/	as in	/edz/ , 'age'	/vekait/ 'vacate'	and	/se/ 'say'
/æ/	as in	/æd/ , 'add'	and	/bæt/ 'bat'	
/ə/	as in	/əbaut/ 'about'	and	/pəteitə/ 'potato'	
/ʌ/	as in	/ʌp/ 'up'	and	/bʌt/ and	'but'
/o/	as in	/opən/ 'open'	and	/rotɪt/ 'rotate'	
/a/	as in	/atγ / , 'otter'	/hat/ 'hot'	and	/spa/ 'spa'

classified by the position of the tongue and their corresponding I.P.A. transcriptions with example words (presented in quotes).

If it were the case that the English language had only the above eight vowels, a complete phonological distinction could be made using the position of the tongue in the oral cavity for each vowel. However, there are six additional vowels, which differ from each other as well as from the eight vowels we presented above. They require additional features to be classified distinctly. These vowels are presented in Table 2.2 and their features are discussed further.

Table 2.2 — Vowels not distinguishable by the position of the tongue alone

Phoneme		I.P.A. transcription and example words			
/ɪ/	as in	/ɪt/ , 'it'	/bɪt/ 'bit'	and	/hɪpɪ/ 'hippie'
/ɛ/	as in	/ɛnd/ 'end'	and	/bɛt/ 'bet'	
/ɚ/	as in	/ɚbeɪn/ , 'urbane'	/pɚport/ 'purport'	and	/sisɚ / 'sister'
/ʊ/	as in	/pʊt/ 'put'			
/ɔ/	as in	/ɔful/ , 'awful'	/bɔt/ 'bought'	and	/pɔ/ 'paw'
/ɝ/	as in	/ɝk/, 'irk'	/bɝd/ 'bird'	and	/bɝ/ 'burr'

2.3.1.2 Degree of muscle tenseness

Distinctions between the vowels with identical specifications, such as /i/ and /ɪ/, and /u/ and /ʊ/, are achieved by an additional articulatory feature known as 'tenseness'. 'Tense' vowels are produced with added muscle tension, whereas what can be termed as 'lax' vowels are produced without such muscle tension. Consider the two vowels /u/ and /ʊ/ in the words 'wooed' /wud/ and 'would' /wʊd/. The vowel /u/ is produced with the feature tenseness, and the vowel /ʊ/ without it, because it is the lax vowel.

The phonologically tense vowels are: /i/, /e/, /ə/, /ɚ/, /u/ and /o/, and their lax counterparts are: /ɪ/, /ɛ/, /(ɛ)/, /(ɝ)/, /ʊ/ and /ɔ/ respectively. The vowels /æ/, /ʌ/ and /ɑ/ are neutral for feature tenseness. As a result of the introduction of feature tenseness, all fourteen vowels are phonologically distinct.

2.3.1.3 Tongue tip curling (retroflex)

All vowels are non-retroflex, with the exception of /ɚ/, as in 'urbane', and /ɝ/, as in 'bird', which are retroflex because their production necessitates the curling of the tip of the tongue.

2.3.1.4 Degree of lip rounding

Some of the fourteen English vowels are accompanied by what is known as lip rounding, whilst others have no such lip rounding and others are neutral. Additional lip rounding produces the round vowels which are: /u/, /ʊ/, /o/, /ɔ/ and /a/ (presented here in descending order of roundness). The unrounded vowels are: /i/, /I/, /e/, /ɛ/ and /æ/; and the neutral vowels are: /ə/, / ɜ /, /ɝ/ and /ʌ/.

With round vowels the position of the tongue is to the back, whereas with unrounded vowels the position of the tongue is to the front.

As previously mentioned, difficulties arise in learning the phonetic representations of the vowels when transcribing ongoing speech, owing to the non-discrete nature of vowel articulation. However, vowel transcription can be perfected by systematically utilising 'key words' that contain each vowel, moving on from one vowel to another.

Nasalisation can occur in English vowels when the vowel is followed by a nasalised consonant. Thus, nasalisation of vowels tends to be allophonic as opposed to phonetic, which is the case with the French language where nasalisation can be used to change the meaning of the word. It is, however, important to include this nasalisation in the synthesis of speech.

2.3.2 Consonant classification

In this section we present two commonly used methods of classifying consonant sounds: (a) by place, and (b) by mode of articulation. Under (a) we have, in turn, six subgroups whereas under (b) we have five subgroups.

2.3.2.1 Classification by place of articulation

(1) *Bilabial*

Bilabial phonemes are all produced at the lips and involve both upper and lower lips, hence their name 'bilabial'. Examples of these are /p/, /b/, /m/, and /w/.

(2) *Labiodental*

The production of these consonants involves contact between lower lip and upper teeth, as in the production of /f/ and /v/.

Labiodental and bilabial consonants are sometimes grouped together as labials.

(3) *Linguadental*

These sounds are produced with the tongue between upper and lower teeth, as in / ð / for 'this' and /θ/ for 'thank'. Sometimes these are referred to as interdentals.

(4) *Alveolar*

This classification refers to sounds which are produced when the tongue contacts the alveolar ridge.

The alveolar ridge seems to be the most natural point of contact for the tongue, which perhaps accounts for the high frequency of sounds produced by this method in many languages of the world. For example, English sounds produced here are /t/, /d/ and /n/. Also, the sounds /s/, /z/, /l/ and /r/ are produced with the tongue in close proximity.

In the four groups (i.e. bilabial, labiodental, linguadental and alveolar) the size of the resonant cavity is much larger behind the point of constriction than in the front. These four groups are therefore sometimes referred to as 'front consonants'.

(5) *Palatal*

These sounds are produced when the body of the tongue is in contact with the palate. The following are examples of palatal sounds and corresponding words:

/sh/ as in 'shut' and 'sugar'.

The speech sound which occurs in measure, pleasure, azure, as opposed to /z/ as in zip.

/ch/ as in 'church', 'trench', etc.

The speech sound which is orthographically represented by 'dg', as in 'budge'.

The speech sound which is present in 'yes', 'use', 'onion', 'joyous', 'toy', these being orthographically represented by 'y' or 'u'.

Note that the resonating cavity behind the point of restriction is reduced with palatal sounds and the cavity is enlarged in front of the point of constriction. These consonants are known as 'back consonants'.

(6) *Velar*

These sounds are produced when the tongue touches, or is near to the velum or soft palate. For example, the sounds /k/, /g/ and /h/, and the sound orthographically represented by 'ng' as in 'sing'.

The examples given above are from the perspective of the English speaker, and certain details may require alteration for other languages. It has been claimed that man is capable of making 26 articulatory points of contact as used in all the languages of the world. This implies that there are many more phonemes and allophones than those we have discussed so far.

2.3.2.2. *Classification by mode of articulation*

Consonants can be categorised according to 'the way' they are articulated. The classifications here are distinctive, in that they are binary and can be used to identify uniquely a given phoneme class. Fig. 2.2 presents the classification of consonants by their mode of articulation. Each class is presented separately below.

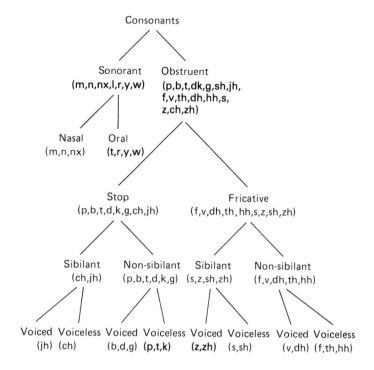

Fig. 2.2 — Classification of consonants by their mode of production.

(1) *Sonorant/obstruent*
This class distinguishes all consonants according to the degree of vocal tract obstruction necessary to produce the sound. Sonorants only require a minimal amount of obstruction whereas obstruents require a considerable amount.

(2) *Nasal/oral*
In this class we distinguish speech sounds on the basis of the resonating cavities used. For oral speech sounds only the oral (not the nasal) cavity is used. For nasal speech sounds the entire vocal tract, including the nasal cavity, is used.

(3) *Stop/fricative*
Both of these require obstruction of the vocal tract and are therefore classed as obstruents. However, stops require a complete closure at a given point in the vocal tract whereas fricative sounds do not.

Stops are also called 'plosives', the term implying the 'explosive release' of the air flow following a stop. These usually occur at the beginning of words or syllables, and as such the term plosive is relevant only to initial stops or syllables.

(4) *Sibilant/non-sibilant*
Sibilancy is distinguished by the prominence of a hissing sound, as for example /s/.

(5) *Voiced/voiceless*
Voicing is distinguished by the presence of vibration in the vocal cords. All sonorants are voiced (as are all vowels) and as such 'voicing' is of little use in categorising these. However, not all obstruents are voiced and hence this category can be used to sub-divide them.

2.4 PHONETIC SUB-DIVISION OF WORDS

Each language has a set of rules governing the sequence in which phonemes can follow each other. If each phoneme could follow any other phoneme with equal probability, there would be no need for 'phonotactics' (i.e. the study of the way the phonemes of a language can combine together). Furthermore, different phoneme combinations are allowed in different languages.

Phonotactic rules are of particular importance from the point of view of continuous speech recognition and synthesis. Evidently, knowledge of allowed phoneme combinations and their probability of occurrence can be beneficial when designing suitable algorithms that reconstruct 'mutilated' phoneme sequences.

Our analysis of a sample English text comprising approximately 70 000 words has shown that the most commonly occurring diphone combination is /dh ax/ (as in the words 'that', 'than', etc.) with a frequency of occurrence of 2.634%.

Frequency statistics on other phonetic subcomponents of words, besides the phoneme, can also provide useful knowledge of the written and spoken language. In this section we discuss three phonetic subdivisions of words: the diphone, the syllable, and the morpheme.

2.4.1 Diphone
The term diphone is used to represent a vowel-consonant sequence such that the segment extends from the centre of the vowel to the centre of the consonant and vice versa. A diphone is sometimes known as a 'transeme' and is a useful concept since some of the allophonic variations are included within the diphone unit.

2.4.2 Syllable
The syllable is intermediate in size between the phone and what is known as the 'morpheme' which we discuss later. The syllable has shown itself as a useful sized element from the point of view of word synthesis, because it overcomes some of the problems of co-articulation at the phoneme level.

The importance of the syllable from the phonetic point of view is that it determines what is permitted and what is not in the phoneme sequence of a language. Once the structure of the monosyllable has been ascertained it is possible to account for all larger units as sequences of syllables. With few exceptions, nothing occurs in these larger units which cannot be accounted for as a result of concatenating single syllables.

The syllable is also convenient in phonology, where there is a hierarchy of units each built up from the next smallest. Our minimum unit is the phone, followed by the phoneme and diphone, and then comes the syllable which is made up of diphone arrangements.

2.4.3 Morpheme
The morpheme is a distinguishable and meaningful linguistic form which is different from others with similar sounds. A morpheme is not usually divided into other forms. For example, the word 'national' contains two morphemes: 'nation' and 'al'; the word 'galactic' has two morphemes: 'galaxy' and 'ic'.

The morpheme is of particular importance for speech synthesis and recognition, because it can form the basis for the creation of a dictionary that contains all the morphemes of a language. The dictionary can then be used as the basis to decompose each incoming word more quickly without having to apply letter-to-phoneme rules.

2.5 SUPRASEGMENTAL FEATURES
2.5.1 Introduction
Athough the phoneme is a useful concept as far as transcribing the spoken word unambiguously is concerned, it is not capable of dealing with other features present in natural language. 'Suprasegmental' features provide us with information on top of the actual words spoken. Such features include word pitch and intonation, word stress, word rhythm and length, and word boundaries.

It has in the past been a 'trend' to regard suprasegmental features as 'fancy optional extras' as far as computer speech synthesis is concerned. However, it can be the lack of these very features that can lead to the rejection of the 'computer voice', along with any information the computer is trying to impart. Examples of this can be seen in everyday life, all of us at some time being sent to sleep by a lecturer's monotonous voice.

Suprasegmental features are very difficult to define and formalise (the rules) from the linguistic point of view. However, given some rules, certain features can be added on to an existing speech synthesis system without too many overheads.

2.5.2 Word pitch and intonation
All languages utilise a varying word pitch which mainly determines differences in meaning. Pitch is produced by variations in the rates of vibration of the vocal cords and is closely related to differences in the fundamental frequency.

In the English language, pitch operates on whole utterences, as for example in the sentence 'You told him' where, if the pitch falls from 'told' to 'him', the effect is that of a statement. However, if it rises, the effect is that of a question: 'You told him?' In this example, the component words are the same and although they are said with differing patterns of pitch, we are still able to recognise them as being the same; it is the interpretation which has been altered.

Single words may also be treated in a similar way, as for example the word 'Yes' as a statement where the pitch falls, and 'Yes?' in the form of a question where the pitch rises. The use of pitch to distinguish whole utterences without interfering with the shape of the component word is known as 'intonation'.

Intonation is defined as 'modulation of the voice in speaking'. It is used to convey the emotions of the speaker as well as additional information. Referring again to the many different ways of saying 'Yes', it depends on the message we want to convey and the situation in which it is said. When said brusquely, 'Yes' can imply 'What do you want, can't you see I am busy?', but when said in a cheerful way it can imply 'Great! I can't think of anything I would like more'.

We also adopt different 'styles' of intonation depending on who we are talking to. The style depends on a number of factors, such as mood, the environment, the topic of discussion, etc. Compare, for example, the way we talk to young children with the way we talk to our manager.

Together with cultural idiosyncracies, intonation can also be used to change the whole meaning of certain sentences or phrases. For example, the statement 'Would you like to come in and see my etchings?' can have two different interpretations, dependent entirely on the circumstances and who is saying it to whom!

With intonation, it is possible to imply the opposite of the actual words spoken. For example, in reponse to the question, 'Did you enjoy the party last night?' you can imply that you had a 'great' time, or that it was a really dreadful party, merely by changing how you say the word 'great'.

In some languages (e.g. Mandarin) intonation can be used to change the meaning of a word (i.e. a word has a completely different meaning with different forms of intonation). This feature is not present in the English language.

Thus, intonation has an important role to play in the communicative process and we must aim to introduce this into voice producing/receiving systems of the future. The difficulty arises from the fact that intonation is very much context-dependent. It would not be difficult, however, to imagine a voice-producing system that adopted appropriate intonation and stressing techniques depending on receiver, age or sex. For example, the output would be modified appropriately for a child or a middle-aged woman.

2.5.3 Word stress

Stress is an important feature in the English language and is an essential part of word shape. Stressed sounds tend to be perceived as being louder (more prominent) than non-stressed sounds.

Stress in the English language depends on pitch, duration of sound and possibly on vowel quality. A syllable has the potential of being accented, but whether it is or not depends on the individual speaker.

Placement of stress relates, to a certain extent, on word shape and so a set of stress assignment rules can be developed. For example, a rule might state: stress the first syllable of a word unless it is a prefix, in which case stress the second syllable. These rules are important for speech synthesis and are applied at the phoneme level.

Stress is particularly important when making an allophonic transcription, since an allophonic variation can depend on the stress placed on the various allophones.

2.5.4   Word rhythm and length

Rhythm in the English language is based on the stressed syllable. Speech is divided up into groups of syllables, each of which contains one and only one stressed syllable. For example, compare the statements 'the man hours' and 'the manpower hours'; the syllables /man/ and /hours/ are stressed in both, but the length of /man/ is far shorter in 'manpower' than in 'man'. This is because there is a tendency for the syllable occurring between stresses to be compressed into the same length of time. We therefore say the word 'manpower' in almost the same time as 'man'. Consequently, the syllable /man/ differs in length between these cases.

The relative lengths of syllables, apart from assisting in the identification of stress, show a grouping together of syllables by a rhythmic principle. This can be used to underline certain syntactic groupings.

The duration of a syllable, word or phone are all variable and can be used for linguistic purposes. For example, the sound /n/ in 'fantastic' can be lengthened to convey extra meaning (e.g. 'fannnnntastic'). Alternatively, it can be of variable length in different words, such as 'bend' and 'bent'; the /n/ being longer in the former word. These variations all pose their own problems as far as speech synthesis and speech recognition are concerned.

2.6   WORD BOUNDARIES

Suprasegmental features are often of importance in detecting word boundaries in continuous speech. We give words a 'shape' by the stress, length and tone we place on the different phonemes/syllables present in the word. In English, for example, we pronounce a given combination of phonemes (consonants and vowels) in a different way when they occur at a word boundary. For example, 'great ape' and 'grey tape' are perceived by the listener to be different due to the different allophones in relation to the word boundary. The /ei/ phoneme is longer in 'great' than in 'grey'. Consequently, stress can also have a role to play in allophonic variation of some English vowels.

The detection of word boundaries is not always as simple as in the above example, and not everything is known about how we recognise them. We also have a tendency to 'merge' the end of one word into the beginning of the next.

Allophonic variations are not confined to individual words but can spread across word boundaries. For example, 'What do you want?' tends to come out as 'Wad jew want?'. These variations again pose problems from the point of view of accurate speech recognition and from the perspective of recreating truly human-sounding speech as opposed to the stilted discrete word production available with present-day voice output systems.

A clearly defined set of rules therefore needs to be developed both for merging words and for unravelling words that are merged.

2.7 PARALINGUISTIC FEATURES

In addition to suprasegmental features, there are the so-called 'paralinguistic features present in every language. These include such things as whispering to indicate secrecy, raising of the voice to indicate anger, etc. These features will become of increasing importance in voice chips aiming for maximum communicative effect.

The problem with paralinguistic features is that there can never be a set of global rules that govern their production, because they are very much context-dependent. Besides, a particular form of paralinguism can extend over a long period of speech and may also be used habitually by a speaker.

2.8 CONCLUSIONS

In conclusion, it must now be apparent that there are many problem areas in continuous speech recognition and production. Some of the problems are being overcome with varying degrees of success but others have yet to be tackled. There are essentialy six problem areas and these are listed below.

(1) *Acoustic-phonetic non-invariance*
The acoustic-phonetic realisations of human speech are context-dependent and even in the same context can receive a large variety of acoustic interpretation.

(2) *Speed of production*
The individual sounds of speech (phones) are pronounced at various speeds, depending both on the context of what is being said and on the speaker. An individual allophone can therefore have diffferent durations in different circumstances.

(3) *Differences between speakers*
The shape and size of the vocal tract varies from one individual to another, as do the vocal cords. This leads to differences in the formant frequencies, pitch, etc. In addition, speakers from different regions tend to adopt distinct phonetic features. We notice this in the different regional accents, (e.g. Welsh, cockney). On top of these variations each individual speaker may use different phonetic features even when pronouncing the same word.

(4) *Phonological recoding*

The way a word is pronounced or 'phonetically realised' is heavily dependent on the sentence and context in which it occurs. There are certain rules which can be applied to obtain the necessary pronunciation. The operational system, incorporating the rules and their phonetic representation, is called phonological recoding.

(5) *Suprasegmental features*

As mentioned before, these features are highly context- and sentence-dependent. They can affect the length of individual allophones and can vary according to the position in which they occur in a word. They can also convey additional information on top of the actual words which a voice recognition system may not be able to recognise.

(6) *Lexical features*

One of the problems here is the so called 'homophone' which defines two or more words that sound the same but have different meanings. Example words here are site, sight and cite. However, they do not usually occur together in the same sentence.

Another problem here is the merging of one word into the next during continuous speech. This poses problems particularly in the speech recognition process.

3

Techniques for digital coding of speech

3.1 INTRODUCTION

The techniques for processing speech signals falls into two main categories: (a) analogue and (b) digital (Rabiner and Schafer, 1978). The techniques for digitising signals can be further subdivided into (b1) waveform coding and (b2) parametric coding (Lee and Lochovsky, 1983); these categories are represented in Fig. 3.1. The distinction between waveform and parametric

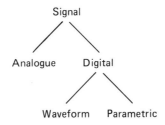

Fig. 3.1 — Classification of processing of speech signals.

coding is made according to whether speech signals are digitised directly and wholly, or are first sampled and only certain signals are extracted and digitised accordingly.

Although the techniques for storing analogue signals are well established, they do not allow flexible and optimal manipulation of speech. It becomes necessary, therefore, to digitise speech by converting analogue signals to digits (zeros and ones). The digits can then be processed accordingly, just like any other data held on computer-readable media. The two most important parameters are the speed of transmission (from analogue to digital and vice versa) and the amount of storage required. The technology has yet to establish the correct balance between the two; the ultimate objective is to reduce the storage requirements without affecting the quality of the reproduced speech.

Under waveform coding, complete utterances are encoded in a manner similar to conventional analogue speech-recording techniques. The most important techniques here are pulse code modulation (P.C.M.), differential pulse code modulation (D.P.C.M.), adaptive differential pulse code modulation (A.D.P.C.M.), and adaptive delta modulation (A.D.M.). Storage requirements with waveform-coding techniques are high, ranging from 17 000 to 70 000 bits per second of encoded speech.

The simplest waveform-coding technique is P.C.M. and requires approximately 64K bit storage per second of speech. The techniques of D.P.C.M. and A.D.M. require between 16 and 32K bits per second of speech. The storage requirements here can be reduced further by taking account of long- and short-term trends of speech signals.

Under parametric coding only certain 'core' signals are extracted, on the basis of a predetermined model of human sounds, and are then processed further. The techniques are called parametric because the parameters adopted (e.g. peak resonances, pitch period, amplitude) are based on the analysis of the human vocal tract and speech articulators such as lips, tongue and jaw. Speech devices which employ parametric coding techniques are otherwise referred to as 'vocal tract synthesisers'.

The grouping of sounds by their acoustic characteristics (e.g. vowels such as /a/, /o/, /e/, and fricatives such as /ch/, /sh/) enables us to sample the signals and to identify peak resonances (otherwise called formants), which are of course related to speech articulators.

Examples of parametric coding techniques are formant coding, channel coding, and linear predictive coding (L.P.C.). The signal rate is between 300 and 10 000 bits per second of speech and therefore these techniques have low storage requirements.

In this chapter we outline the most commonly used techniques for digitisation, together with some of the data compression techniques employed (Cappellini, 1985). First we discuss analogue storage and the reasons it has been mostly superseded by digital storage in speech synthesis and recognition systems.

3.2 ANALOGUE STORAGE

This method stores an analogue representation of the sound wave. However, its use for computerisation has been found unsuitable because (a) it is difficult to access different utterances quickly, and (b) even though random-access tape-recorders can be used they are expensive and prone to mechanical breakdown because of the stress placed on them.

A mechanical drum has also been used to store analogue representations of speech, but it has proved difficult to generate correct sounding speech by concatenating words from the store. The problem here is that sounds recorded in isolation or in a different context from the one being used do not sound natural. This is the result of incorrect placement of stress, intonation, etc., which has been shown to lead to the loss of word recognition.

Photographic film can be used, as in the case of the original speaking clock, but again the speech does not sound natural.

Analogue signals are prone to noise interference and distortion, whereas digits can be stored in an electronic memory without corruption. It is also difficult to store an analogue signal without some deterioration. For example, magnetic tape is subject to wear and stretching.

3.3 DIGITAL STORAGE

3.3.1 Introduction

Digital systems were first designed to simulate analogue ones and have been found to be both reliable and compact. Additionally, the data are in a form which is easy to transmit and process in the same way as other digital information. Furthermore, solid-state electronics are much cheaper than the mechanical means of storing speech as outlined above.

As stated before, digital storage techniques can be subdivided into two classes: (a) waveform and (b) parametric. However, both techniques involve storing a series of binary digits to represent the incoming sound wave. The digits are obtained by sampling the sound wave and performing an analysis in order to obtain some form of binary representation of its changing 'shape' (Jayant and Noll, 1984).

Digital signal processing is concerned both with obtaining discrete representations of the signal and with the various mathematical methods for processing and implementing the results.

When an analogue signal is converted to a digital equivalent, a record has to be made both of the amplitude and the associated time. Compare this to the process of plotting a graph where we start off with a list of values, mark the appropriate place on the graph and then join up the marks to form a continuous curve. When digitising an analogue signal we are in effect performing the reverse of the graph-drawing process, that is, we obtain sufficient X, Y coordinates to enable us to reproduce accurately the original curve. The analogue signal is first sampled and the samples are then converted to a digital form.

3.3.2 Digital sampling

The first question to answer is 'How often do we need to take the samples in order to obtain an accurate representation of the sound wave?' For example, if we take the sample at time periods which coincide with the fundamental frequency for a given sound wave, then very little information would be obtained.

It has been demonstrated that a signal can be reconstructed accurately from a sampled version, only if it does not contain components whose frequency is greater than half the frequency at which the sampling takes place. Therefore, before sampling a signal, we must ensure that no significant sound waves are present with a frequency greater than half the sample frequency. In other words, the rate at which the sample is taken (sample frequency) must be at least twice the frequency of the highest frequency of interest (i.e. the highest frequency of all those being sampled).

The sampling of frequencies can be illustrated by using the telephone as an example. The telephone exchange aims to transmit frequencies lower than 3.4 kHz. This frequency range contains all the information-bearing formants and some of the aspiration energy. For the telephone, the sampling frequency must be at least 6.8 kHz, although in practice speech contains significant components with a frequency above 3.4 kHz, with the result that speech requires filtering prior to sampling. If this is not done the higher frequencies lead to distortion of the lower frequencies.

In practice, sampling rates above the bare minimum are normally used because it is not possible to make a perfect filter. In addition, if the sampling rate is not high enough, something known as 'aliasing' can occur, having an undesirable effect. With aliasing, when the signal is changed back into an analogue signal using the stored digits, some components are introduced which were not in the original signal.

3.3.3 Digitisation

Having taken the sample, it is necessary to find some means of digitising the amplitude. If the electronic circuit used has 12 bits available it is possible to store any number up to 4096 in its binary form. Generally, a 12-bit converter is good enough for the vast majority of applications, although an 8-bit converter is satisfactory in most cases.

One method of digitisation quantises the amplitude range into equal regions, where the points are termed 'quantisation levels', each having a binary number associated with it. Half of the levels will be needed for positive inputs and the other for negative inputs. The amplitude of the sample taken is then compared with these 'quantisation levels' and rounded down to the nearest level. It is the binary representation of this level that is then stored.

Fig. 3.2(a) shows an example analogue wave and Fig. 3.2(b) shows the samples taken at the sampling frequency. The samples are then quantised, resulting in a number of allowed amplitude values (see Fig. 3.2(c)), which can then be represented in binary form.

The accuracy of conversion consequently depends on the number of levels present; the more levels there are, the more accurate the conversion then becomes. The number of levels is chosen so as to give the required accuracy when there are low-amplitude signals (e.g. in the case of speech that corresponds to a quiet speaker).

A problem now arises with the size of the computer memory needed to store all the digits generated. Assuming a sample frequency of 10 000 samples per second (this is not unreasonable for speech) and the use of an 8-bit converter, then for one second of speech 80 000 bits will be required.

Considering the fact that the average rate of phoneme production is approximately 10 to 15 phonemes per second, it is apparent that a considerable amount of memory is necessary to store even short conversations. Various digitising techniques aim to overcome this problem by reducing the number of bits required. This is achieved by removing any redundant information without affecting the quality of the reproduced speech signal.

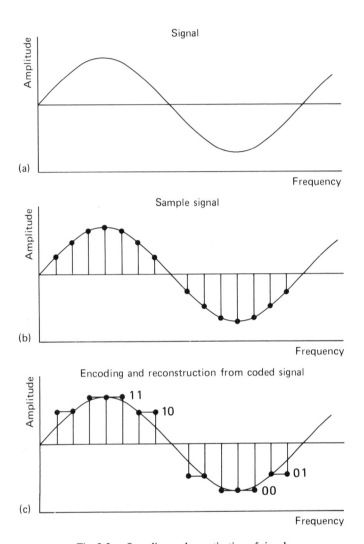

Fig. 3.2 — Sampling and quantisation of signals.

The famous mathematical theory of communication first introduced by Shannon in 1948 (Shannon, 1948; Shannon and Weaver, 1949), aims to quantify the amount of information that is stored and transmitted through channels which may or may not have memory.

Generally, a symbol for transmission will be selected from a set of possible symbols which can be letters, words, sentences, complete messages, musical notes, etc. For example, a complete set of symbols could be the English alphabet (A to Z).

If certain rules are in operation when a symbol is selected, making some choices more likely than others, then Shannon's theory of communication provides a measure of the degree of freedom of choice available. In the English language, there are grammatical rules which increase the likelihood of certain choices being made, where the probability of one word following another depends on the preceding choices. There are also rules operating within words, based for example on the fact that certain letter combinations occur more frequently than others (e.g. the letters 'th' occur more frequently than 'qu'), and some never occur (e.g. 'zq'). Shannon's theory (Shannon, 1948) provides a measure of this 'freedom' of choice.

The term 'information' in communication theory is not related to semantics, that is, the meaning of of messages, data, etc., but rather to what you could say. It refers to the atomic quantities necessary and sufficient to represent (codify) data of any sort.

'Entropy' is a term often used in information theory (Bell, 1968) to refer to the degree of randomness exhibited by a system. Information is in fact measured by entropy. When the entropy is low, we have a limited choice and the system is highly organised. Conversely, when the entropy is high there are more choices available, each being nearly equiprobable, and the system shows a high degree of randomness. The entropy of an ensemble can be calculated using the following well-established formula:

$$H = -\sum_{i=1}^{N} p_i \log p_i$$

where p_i is the probability of each symbol and N is the total number of distinct symbols processed.

The 'redundancy' of the system as a whole (i.e. $1-H$) is that fraction of a 'message' which is determined not by the free choice of the 'sender', but rather by the accepted statistical rules governing the symbols in question. That is, by knowing the rules and the symbol set, we can predict certain events (choices). Thus, time and storage space can be saved by excluding those symbols which can be predicted accurately.

3.3.4   Data compression techniques

The basic components of a digital communication link are presented in Fig. 3.3. The task performed by each of these is as follows:

(a)   The source generating the samples which have already been quantised and encoded in a finite alphabet (e.g. the binary system).
(b)   The source encoder that codes the signals and reduces the amount of redundancy.
(c)   The channel encoder that encodes the signals and prepares them for transmission (reintroducing a certain amount of redundancy in many cases, in order to recover from errors in the transmission caused by noise or other interferences (Shannon and Weaver, 1949)).
(d)   The actual channel.
(e)   The channel decoder that reverses the process of (c) above.

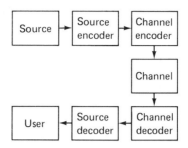

Fig. 3.3 — Basic components of a digital communication link.

(f)   The source decoder that reconstructs the original signal.
(g)   The receiver that accepts the signals transmitted originally.

The mathematical theory of communication has been extensively applied to the above communication system and has made possible the design of many efficient algorithms for storing and transmitting data effectively.

In order to achieve efficient transmission, redundancy in the transmitted data has to be reduced as much as possible; clearly, data which contains no redundancy cannot be further compressed.

There are many algorithms for achieving efficient data compression (Cappellini, 1985). In many of these we need to know the source output statistics to design efficient and optimal algorithms. However, in most practical situations these statistics are not known or are not stationary. This results in difficulty in designing optimal algorithms which remain efficient during the evolution of the signal with time. There are, however, many algorithms which do not need exact knowledge of the source statistics to achieve a good performance. In this section we outline some of these algorithms.

There are various algorithms which can be split into two main classifications: (a) predictors, and (b) interpolators (Campanella, 1976). These are generally very easy to implement on hardware and have therefore been used extensively.

Predictors utilise past knowledge of previous samples, whereas interpolators utilise both past and future samples. Generally, a tolerance band is placed around the estimated value. If the current value falls within a specific tolerance band, it is considered to be redundant and its value is not transmitted. In order to be able to reconstruct the original data from the transmitted data, the non-redundant samples have time/position identification added. This is achieved by storing the non-redundant samples in a buffer, before transmission, and then inserting the neccesary data. Thus, the buffer can store the incoming signals so that they can be sent out at a uniform rate.

3.3.4.1 Predictors
Zero-order predictors

In zero-order predictors only the last sample is used to predict the current sample. In the 'fixed aperture' mode, the range of the data is subdivided into a set of fixed bands. If the predicted and actual values fall within the same band, then the prediction is considered to have succeeded and the value is not transmitted.

In the 'floating aperture' mode, the tolerance bands can be made variable by placing the tolerance band around the last transmitted sample. This leads to a more flexible algorithm.

First order predictors

In first-order predictor algorithms two samples are utilised to predict the current sample. The first two samples are transmitted and a straight line is drawn between the two. A tolerance band is then placed about the obtained line. If the next sample (in this case the third) is within this tolerance band, then the prediction has succeeded and the data is not transmitted. If the prediction fails, the data is transmitted and a new straight line is drawn which utilises this transmitted value.

The algorithm here can be modified to reduce the effects of channel noise by transmitting the last predicted value each time the prediction fails. This method strongly reduces the distortion produced by channel noise.

Predictors of higher order than one are seldom used in practical applications as they are often unstable and very sensitive to any disturbance/noise.

Linear predictors

The speech signal has a degree of regularity over short stretches and this regularity can form the basis of some sort of prediction, with a certain degree of accuracy. One such method was devised by Kolmogorov in the forties. He devised a very general polynomial in which the next sample is predicted as the sum of a large number of terms containing previous samples. The polynomial used has the following form:

$$s(n) = \sum_{i=1}^{M} c(i)\, s(n-i)$$

where $s(n)$ is the predicted value of the nth sample based on the previous samples $s(n-M)$, $s(n-1-M)...s(n-1)$. The values $c(i)$, $c(i-1)...$ are constant coefficients that have to be determined by statistical analysis. Note that the predictor we discuss here plays the role of a filter representing the filtering action of the vocal tracts.

The basic steps of the algorithm proposed by Kolmogorov are as follows each sample is multiplied by a constant coefficient (linear terms), the samples are then taken in pairs and multiplied together (quadratic terms), in threes and multiplied together (cubic terms), and so on. Predictive speech devices use only the linear terms (hence the term linear prediction (L.P.C.)) (Makhoul, 1975) since the use of more terms can be computationally time-consuming.

The constant coefficients are selected so as to minimise the error between the predicted value and the actual value. This can be done using a variety of numerical methods. In order to obtain the best results, some form of statistical analysis needs to be carried out on the expected input and, if possible, input from the speaker concerned. From the analysis, a set of coefficients are generated which will then be used in the predictor algorithm to give an optimum performance. If on the other hand the input statistics are not known and an arbitrary set of coefficients is chosen, the quality of the resultant reconstructed speech can be plagued with two types of error: slope overload and granular noise (these are discussed later).

There are many different ways of implementing the basic idea behind linear prediction. For example, there is 'feed forward' prediction, where the output is the predicted next sample based on the linear combination of the previous samples. Another example is 'feedback' prediction, where a set of samples is used to predict the sample immediately before the first sample of a set. The complexity of the system as a whole depends on what form the predictor algorithm takes.

In conclusion, linear prediction algorithms can be broadly classed as adaptive or non-adaptive, depending on the amount and degree of knowledge the algorithm possesses about the speech process as a whole.

Adaptive predictors

In many cases sufficient knowledge of the source statistics is not available. This means that it is difficult to determine the fixed predictor coefficients utilised in the last examples (zero-order, first-order and linear predictors). In these cases, it is often convenient to utilise a predictor algorithm which can be adapted accordingly. With adaptive algorithms the prediction coefficients are changed according to how the signal evolves with time. Adaptive and asynchronous prediction techniques are discussed below in more detail.

(a) Adaptive prediction

Here, a learning capability is introduced into the predictor algorithms we discussed previously. For example, in linear prediction the coefficients are determined in order to minimise the mean squared error of the predicted sample values. In addition, a weighting coefficient is incorporated into the formula in order to assign a relative importance to each part of the predictor.

(b) Asynchronous prediction

With this type of algorithm, the length of the 'prediction interval' is determined by the signs and values of the past p differences between the predicted and the actual values. If the past p differences have a maximum value and the same sign, then the prediction frequency is *increased* by a factor x. Alternatively, if they have alternating signs ($-+-+-$, etc.), the prediction frequency is *decreased* by a factor x. The problem here is how to determine the best value for p and x through a set of tests.

Adaptive algorithms are generally more complex to implement but have a reasonable performance for a large class of signals.

3.3.4.2   *Interpolators*

These predicting algorithms differ from those discussed previously because they utilise both past and future samples to perform the prediction of the current sample. There are many algorithms under this classification; we discuss zero-order and first-order interpolators.

Zero-order interpolators

Here, a tolerance band is placed about the first and the second samples, giving rise to one of the following two cases:

(a)   the two tolerance bands can have parts in common (intersection band);

(b)   The bands have no parts in common.

Under (a) the first sample can be represented by the mean value of the intersection band, with an error equal to less than half the tolerance band, and as a result the first sample is not transmitted. The third sample is then taken into account and a tolerance band is placed about it. If this tolerance band has a part in common with the previous intersection band, the second sample is considered to have been correctly predicted. In this case (correct prediction) a new intersection band is formed, as the intersection between the tolerance bands placed around the first, second and third samples. At the receiver the redundant samples (non-transmitted) are replaced by the mean value of the intersection bands.

Under (b) the first sample is transmitted and utilised as the first point for the next prediction. This process is then repeated until all the signals have been transmitted.

First-order interpolators

In first-order interpolators the prediction of the actual sample is performed using straight lines. There are two basic steps:

Step 1: Draw two straight lines from the first sample (n) to the limits of the tolerance band for the second sample ($n+1$) and thereby form an angle θ as shown below:

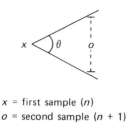

x = first sample (n)
o = second sample $(n + 1)$

Step 2: Draw two straight lines from the first sample (n) to the limits of the tolerance band for the third sample $(n+2)$ and thereby form an angle α as shown below:

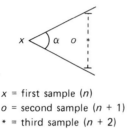

x = first sample (n)
o = second sample $(n + 1)$
$*$ = third sample $(n + 2)$

If the two angles θ and α have a non-zero intersection angle, the second sample is considered to have been predicted correctly and the second sample is not then transmitted. This process continues until a prediction fails. The process will then start again utilising either $n+1$ (in this case the second) or $n+2$ (in this case the third) sample as the first point in the prediction chain.

If the sample $n+1$ is used, the method is termed 'joined line segment method'. If the sample $n+2$ is used, it is termed 'the disjoined line segment method'. The disjoined line segment method has the advantage over the joined line segment method in that it is more stable and less sensitive to channel errors.

3.4 WAVEFORM CODING AND PARAMETRIC CODING

There are various techniques for converting an analogue signal to a digital equivalent. These techniques often employ some form of a compression algorithm such as the ones we discussed in the previous section. As already discussed, the techniques for processing speech signals fall into two major categories: (a) waveform coding, and (b) parametric coding. Each of these is now discussed in more detail below.

3.4.1   Waveform Coding

In this technique the whole of the sound wave is digitised directly, aiming to preserve all the necessary features present in the original analogue speech signal. Some of the most important techniques in this area are:

(a)   Pulse code modulation
(b)   Differential pulse code modulation
(c)   Adaptive differential pulse code modulation
(d)   Delta modulation
(e)   Adaptive delta modulation
(f)   The Mozer method

The disadvantage of these techniques is that the storage requirements are high, ranging from 17 000 to 70 000 bits per second of speech.

3.4.1.1   Pulse code modulation (P.C.M.)

This is the most bit-consuming digitising process but it is also the most established and most applied of all the digital coding techniques. One of the reasons for this is that it is one of the earliest digitising techniques developed and one of the best understood because of its conceptual simplicity. Other advantages are that it is instantaneous, with a coding delay of no more than one sample period, and in addition it is not signal-specific, unlike differential pulse code modulation.

All waveform coding techniques, with the possible exception of delta modulation, involve some form of P.C.M.

The code in P.C.M. refers to the fact that the information in the stored bits is a special code-word, that is, the signal is quantised, an appropriate code-word is generated and subsequently stored. If for example, 2 bits per sample are required, then each input amplitude is quantised into $2^2=4$ possible levels. These could be: 20, 10, -10, -20; such levels could be represented by code-words 00, 01, 10 and 11 respectively. If, as is the case in the above example, there is a very coarse quantisation, there will be a large occurrence of reconstruction errors. Obviously, the more bits we have available the finer the quantisation levels become.

P.C.M. analyses and reconstructs a waveform by taking into account only the bandwidth of the waveform, not the underlying structure. As a result, complete messages can be generated, although it is not always possible to create new phrases, messages, etc. by concatenating the ones held in memory.

3.4.1.2   Differential pulse code modulation (D.P.C.M.)

This is a technique which can use any of the prediction techniques we discussed previously in order to anticipate the incoming signal. For example, linear prediction can be used and coding bit rates as low as 800 bits per second can be obtained.

Although D.P.C.M. achieves better data compression than P.C.M., it does have its overheads, particularly the cost of implementing the algorithm. This is due to the fact that any digitising technique which implements some form of prediction must utilise adders, multipliers and delay elements for storing previous samples.

With D.P.C.M. the difference between the incoming and the predicted signal is quantised in steps of amplitude and encoded for transmission. Since the technique depends on knowledge of the speech process in order to predict the incoming signal, it is restricted (in the present context) to speech signals. This is not the case with P.C.M. which is not signal-specific.

As the difference in amplitude is quantised in fixed steps, two basic forms of reconstruction error can occur: (a) slope overload, and (b) granular noise. Under (a) the step size is too small for the incoming wave, as might be the case for a high-frequency high-amplitude signal. In this case the size of the steps are going to be too small and the integrator is not going to be able to follow the slope accurately. In extreme cases a sign wave could end up as a triangular wave. Alternatively, if the step size is too large the result may well be granularity.

To avoid these two types of error three strategies can be adopted:

(a)   Use of adaptive quantisation of the step amplitude;
(b)   The use of adaptive prediction;
(c)   Varying the sample frequency.

These are now discussed under adaptive differential pulse code modulation.

3.4.1.3 Adaptive differential pulse code modulation (A.D.P.C.M.)

This is a technique for digitising speech signals and is similar to D.P.C.M., but whereas in D.P.C.M. the predictor has been chosen to give optimum performance and is fixed, in A.D.P.C.M. the predictor or 'step' size can be altered to take into account the 'shape' of the predicted signal. This is called 'adaptive quantisation', where the step size is small when the signal is varying slowly and large when it is varying quickly. This means that the contours of the speech signal can be followed more readily.

The adaption of the step size can be carried out according to several different algorithms. These usually operate in response to a pattern in the transmitted bits. For example, three consecutive samples with the same value would indicate a slope overload and the step size might be doubled, tripled, etc., depending on the algorithm used. Alternatively, a varying sequence would indicate a well-matched signal.

The step size is chosen so as to give an optimum performance in a given set of circumstances. Since the step size is variable it becomes necessary to be able to derive the step size at the receiver. If, for example, linear prediction is used, it is possible to have 'feed-forward' or 'backward' prediction.

In feed-forward prediction, the code-words and step size together serve as a representation of the signal. In backward prediction, the step size is derived from the code sequence, which means that no additional step size information need be transmitted or stored. Backward prediction has the disadvantage that it is more error prone in transmission than feed-forward prediction. It therefore becomes necessary to transmit/store both the code-word and the step size in order to reconstruct the original signal accurately.

A.D.P.C.M. has the advantage over D.P.C.M., in that the optimum fixed predictor is more likly to be very dependent on speaker and material, whereas A.D.P.C.M. is inherently less so.

Finally, alternative forms of prediction can be used, for example the adaptive and the asynchronous prediction techniques we discussed previously.

3.4.1.4 Delta modulation (D.M.)

This technique is an important subclass of D.P.C.M., utilising only one-bit quantisers (Nuggehally, 1974). With D.M. the changes in the signal ampli-tude between consecutive samples are transmitted in place of the absolute signal amplitude. The fact that these have only a one-bit code-word eliminates the need for word framing (i.e. the decomposition of the bit-stream into fixed units corresponding to the length of the code-word) at the point of transmission/reception. This, and the simplicity of the approach, make D.M. a very attractive method for digital voice storage. Note that, bit rates between 32 and 48 kilobits per second have been achieved with delta modulation.

Basically, a delta modulator consists of an integrator which produces a voltage that can steadily decrease or increase, and a comparable circuit which compares the incoming analogue signal with the output from the integrator. A clock is used to determine the bit transmission rate. If at a clock period the incoming signal is more positive than the integrator output, then a 1 bit is transmitted and the integrator is set in the positive direction. If, on the other hand, the incoming signal is more negative, a 0 bit is transmitted and the integrator is set in the opposite direction. Thus, the incoming signal can be followed and subsequently reconstructed from the series of zeros and ones.

The integrator uses a form of linear prediction, as was the case with the D.P.C.M. we discussed earlier. The problem again arises regarding the choice of an appropriate step size. For example, even if the global input statistics are known and an average is calculated, it would prove impossible to match the step size to the local input at all times. If the input statistics are not known and an arbitrary step size is chosen, the the two extreme cases are repeated, namely slope overload and granularity.

We illustrate some cases with different step sizes and their effect on the resulting coded signal. Fig. 3.4(a) shows a well-matched wave and step size. Fig. 3.4(b) shows a small step size resulting in a triangular wave. Fig. 3.4(c) shows a step-size that is too large, resulting in granularity. Finally Fig. 3.4(d) shows both slope overload and granular noise. Therefore, the choice of step size is a compromise between the two. Obviously, a form of adaptive quantisation would greatly improve the performance of a delta modulator.

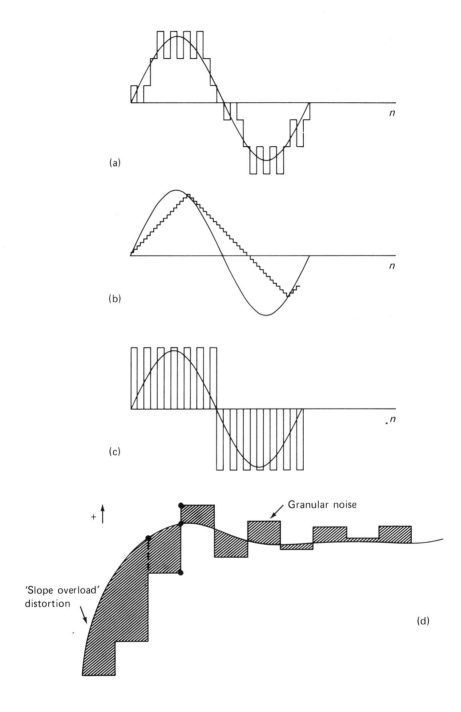

Fig. 3.4 — Examples of step size: (a) a well-matched wave; (b) a case where step size is too small; (c) a case where step size is too big; (d) a case showing slope overload and granular noise.

3.4.1.5 Adaptive delta modulation (A.D.M)

In adaptive delta modulation, as with A.P.C.M., both the amplitude of the step and the sample frequency can be altered. Several methods under the broad area of A.D.M. have been proposed to adapt the amplitude of the step to the dynamic distribution of the signal.

Delta modulation algorithms can be grouped into three classes, depending on the approach adopted to vary the amplitude of the step, as follows.

(1) *Instantaneous compounding.*
Here, the amplitude of the step is evaluated at any instant according to a fixed rule based on the sequence of the previous pulse signals. Two example techniques under this classification are:

  (i) high information delta modulation (H.I.D.M.)
 (ii) Constant factor delta modulation (C.F.D.M.).

In H.I.D.M. the step size is increased in response to consecutive pulses having the same value (e.g. if $n=3$ and there are three consecutive pluses $(+++)$, then the step size is increased).

In C.F.D.M. the sign of the previous and actual sample is the criterion used to decide whether to change the step size or not.

(2) *Syllabic compounding.*
An example here is typified by the so called continuously varying slope delta modulation (C.V.S.D.M.). In C.V.S.D.M. the occurrence of equal consecutive plus signs again indicates slope overload.

(3) *Hybrid compounding*
This is a technique which is frequently used in speech processing. The step amplitude n is given by the following formula:

$$\Delta_n = \Delta_{(n-1)}\, \delta_n$$

where δ_n is the instantaneous step amplitude, computed according to a law depending on the particular application. The initial value thus obtained (Δ_0) is periodically recomputed at syllabic intervals (T), according to the average slope energy (E), during the preceding interval (T), by the formula:

$$\Delta_0 = cE$$

where c is a pre-fixed constant, the value of which must be chosen with care. If c is greater than 1, then the signal may well be found to be unstable. If c is less than 1, then the resulting signal may be close to zero, regardless of the degree of amplitude.

Finally, when adaptivity is achieved by changing the sampling period, the delta modulation is called adaptive asynchronous delta modulation

(A.A.D.M.). The criteria used in A.A.D.M. for determining the sample frequency are mainly the same as those used to determine the amplitude of the step. During high activity, the sampling frequency needs to be rapid, while in periods of low activity the frequency needs to be slower. Fig. 3.5(a)

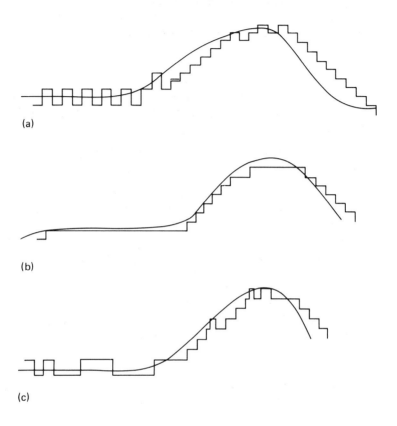

Fig. 3.5 — Examples of A.A.D.M.: (a) a well-matched delta modulator; (b) an ideal A.A.D.M.; (c) a practical A.A.D.M.

shows conventional delta modulation, Fig. 3.5(b) shows the ideal behaviour of an adaptive asynchronous delta modulator, and Fig. 3.5(c) shows the behaviour of a practical adaptive asynchronous delta modulator, where the information about sampling time need not be sent to the receiver.

3.4.1.6 The Mozer technique
The above five methods — P.C.M, D.P.C.M., A.D.P.C.M., D.M. and A.D.M. — are often referred to as 'time waveform' techniques because the whole of the signal is digitised, and the stored or transmitted data represent a compressed waveform as a function of time. In addition, all of these techniques can be applied to other types of analogue signals, such as TV

signals. The Mozer method differs in this respect as it applies only to speech signals.

It is often mistakenly thought that the aim of time waveform techniques is to approximate the original signal as closely as possible but with the lowest number of bits. Rather, the aim is to enable the production of a synthetic waveform from the stored digits, which will be perceived by the listener (in the case of speech) to be the same as the original.

The basic idea behind the Mozer technique is to extract only the relevant information from the signal. Thus, the synthetic waveform may not necessarily bear any resemblence to the original signal when analysed spectrographically.

In the Mozer technique the speech waveform is divided into basic segments called 'analysis periods'. For voiced speech, the analysis period is equal to the period of the vocal cord vibration, while for unvoiced speech the analysis period is taken to be a fixed number of input samples — usually 256. Each type of analysis period is then replaced with a smaller fixed number of samples, making the digital analysis and reconstruction easier, as well as yielding a reduction in the data rate.

Various data compression techniques are then applied to each type of analysis period. For example, the amplitude can be scaled and phases adjusted. Each type of analysis period (voiced/unvoiced) is analysed and compressed in a different manner depending on the differences in their spectra. Data rates of around 1000 bits per second have been obtained using this method.

One of the problems with the more conventional digitising techniques is that for speech synthesis systems (discussed in Chapter 5), it is desirable to be able to change the pitch/intonation patterns present in the stored signal. This is impossible with the more conventional time waveform techniques. The Mozer technique overcomes the problem of intonation, pitch, etc., by introducing periods of silence with varying lengths into the reconstituted digital waveform. By lengthening the periods of silence between sampling periods a falling pitch is simulated, and by shortening the periods of silence a rising pitch is simulated.

3.4.2 Parametric coding

There is a large amount of information present in the acoustic signal, not all of which is necessary for the understanding of the intended message. In waveform coding the signal is processed in such a way as to ignore anything we know about the speech process. For example, we know that vowels produce formants which tend to be concentrated in specific frequency regions, or that speech can be produced with or without voicing. Parametric coding aims to remove some of the redundancies present by encoding only certain core signals (i.e. by extracting certain parameters). These core signals are extracted on the basis of known human sounds, derived from the analysis of the human vocal tract and articulatory organs. Examples of these techniques include (a) channel coding, (b) formant coding and (c) linear predictive coding.

The advantages of these techniques are the low storage requirements and the low bit rate (e.g. 300 to 10 000 bits per second, of speech). It is worth noting that the lower the rate, the more complicated the coder becomes in order to achieve satisfactory speech production. Also, the lower the speed the less natural the 'voice' then sounds. However, the costs of system design (e.g. fewer logic gates), transmission and storage decrease accordingly. Fig. 3.6 shows an approximate spectrum for digital coding of speech. The higher

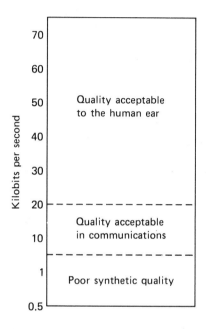

Fig. 6 — Speed of coding techniques and quality.

the rate of sampling (measured in kilobits per second) the better the quality of the reproduced speech.

We now discuss some of the methods available to covert a signal into its frequency domain. These methods extract certain features present in a signal prior to their digitisation; an example of a feature is the pitch.

3.4.2.1   The vocoder
The oldest form of channel-coding device is the vocoder operating at speeds usually less than 6.0 kilobits per second. The rate at which samples are taken (i.e. the frame rate) takes advantage of the fact that speech remains relatively constant over short periods of time. This is because the articulatory organs cannot make leaps from one position to the next. However, there are certain rapid events in speech, such as plosives and stop consonants, which require a rapid response. These cannot be reproduced in channel-coding systems with frame rates below 50 Hz.

Channel-coding techniques digitise speech signals by passing the source signal through a series of filters in parallel. Each filter processes the amplitude and its associated frequency band, and utilises a technique to determine whether the signal is voiced or not. The sound wave is therefore split into a number of frequency bands. A series of figures will be generated to represent the energy in each band, together with information on whether it is voiced or unvoiced, as well as the fundamental frequency. The original signal can be reconstituted from this information.

The information obtained from each band controls the amplitude of the contribution these bands make to the whole. The voiced/unvoiced information is used to select an appropriate excitation generator. Random noise is selected for unvoiced speech but a periodic pulse is selected for voiced speech, the fundamental frequency of the pulse generator being controlled by the pitch signal.

The channel vocoder permits modification to the speech signal at the point of synthesis, since the excitation and vocal tract information are represented separately. Thus, it is possible to change the pitch independently of the vocal tract information. If, for example, the same fundamental frequency is always used (i.e. the pitch information is not utilised) then monotone speech is obtained. If on the other hand random noise is always used, whispered speech is obtained.

The fact that the pitch and the fundamental frequency are stored separately are extremely attractive from the point of view of speech synthesis. This means that intonation, stress, etc., can be added separately to the words for synthesis, which should, in theory, lead to more natural-sounding speech.

One of the weaknesses of the channel vocoder is the fact that the detection of pitch and voicing is not always easy. There is often no clearly defined boundary between voiced and unvoiced sections, and this affects the quality of the synthesis because the synthesised speech can be only pure voiced or pure unvoiced. Consequently, this gives a synthetic quality, which is generally well below the performance obtained by the better waveform-coding techniques.

One of the main advantages of the vocoder is the fact that the data rate is well below that of waveform-coding techniques; the typical range for vocoders is 1 to 3 kilobits per second. However, the problem with this approach is that it is necessary to have a sampling rate which is at least twice as large as the maximum frequency of the incoming analogue signal. Hence, the number of bits per second necessary to represent speech is related to the range of the signals. In addition, a fast processor is needed to cope with the volume of the required data and the large number of calculations involved.

The simplest and the cheapest method of converting a speech signal into a frequency domain is to count the number of times per second a signal changes algebraic sign. This is achieved by means of a special circuit known as a 'zero crossing detector'. The zero-crossing density can contribute to the process that determines whether the signal is voiced or unvoiced. Further, it can be utilised in speech recognition systems to determine where segmentation of the incoming signal can reliably take place. Thus, a zero-crossing density circuit can be incorporated into many different types of frequency domain recognition/synthesis systems. In addition it can be used as a coding technique in its own right, when it is difficult to determine the underlying acoustic and articulatory effects.

3.4.2.2 Formant coding

The basic channel vocoder does not make use of the formant structure of voiced speech sounds, where energy is concentrated in three or four frequency bands known as formants. By making use of this information, it is possible to reduce the redundancy in the transmitted signal still further. In order to do this the formant frequencies have to be extracted, but the analysis process becomes more complex than is the case with the vocoder.

A more sophisticated version of the zero-crossing density technique employs filters to decompose the speech signal into a number of frequency bands (e.g. 200(900Hz, 800(2500Hz and 2000(3200Hz; these are the formant frequencies). Note that the more filters we use the higher the performance will be, but the associated cost increases. By counting the zero crossings separately under each band, it is possible to approximate the corresponding formant frequencies. This method achieves fairly reliable classification of vowel sounds, and has proved to be reasonably successful at word recognition when only small vocabularies are used. Its main advantage is that it is cheap in comparison to some of the other techniques available.

Filtering can also be accomplished with a method known as the 'fast Fourier transform' (F.F.T.). The F.F.T. is an alternative (but computationally quicker) way of solving Fourier transform series. Here, the fundamental frequencies and their associated harmonics are generated mathematically, and subsequently the speech spectrum is obtained. This information is stored digitally, with the fundamental frequency being the parameter associated with voicing. Note that the F.F.T. approach is also used instead of filters in many parametric methods.

3.4.2.3 Linear predictive coding (L.P.C.)

The theory of linear prediction is highly developed, and a large range of techniques pertinent to speech processing have evolved. The techniques have been used in a wide variety of speech-related applications, for example speech recognition (Atal and Hanauer, 1971), speaker verification and identification (Atal, 1974), and others. In addition, linear predictive methods have been formulated for estimating all the basic speech parameters, such as pitch, formants, spectra, and vocal tract area functions. These general techniques are often referred to collectively as 'linear predictive coding' (L.P.C.).

A predictor of any type can also be used as a filter by separating those components it can predict from those it cannot. The prediction error can be obtained by subtracting the actual value from the predicted value. For vowels in particular, the spectrum of the error signal is approximately flat, because the effects of the formants have been eliminated. This means that the error signal can be utilised to extract pitch information: the error signal exhibits sharp pulses corresponding to the pitch periods of the vowels. However, this alone is not always sufficient to be relied upon exclusively, since sounds which are not rich in harmonics (as for example in /m/), do not always give sharp peaks. Consequently, the pulses are not always easy to locate.

A linear predictor can represent the filtering action of the vocal tract by comparing the input and output signals, the difference being the glottal waveform that drives the vocal tract filter. This principle can therefore be utilised to extract the fundamental frequency, and has also been found to be of particular importance when obtaining the formant trajectories.

Formants can also be estimated from the voiced portions of speech by utilising linear prediction analysis. The most direct way is to factorise the predictor polynomial and, based on the roots obtained, to try to determine the formants. Alternatively, the spectrum can be obtained and the formants chosen using a 'peak picking' method.

Another important application of linear predictive analysis has been in the encoding of speech signals for transmission and storage. This is accomplished by what is known as a 'linear predictor coding vocoder'. Generally, the incoming signal is analysed in such a way that the information stored is that which is necessary to synthesise the speech signal, rather than the actual signal itself.

A linear prediction coder consists of a transmitter, which carries out (a) the L.P.C. analysis and pitch detection, and (b) the coding of the parameters for transmission. It also includes a channel to send the appropriately coded parameters, and a receiver which can decode the parameters and use these to synthesise speech. The basic features looked at, in this process, are (a) the pitch period, (b) the voiced/unvoiced parameter, and (c) the gain parameter. (Note that the gain control determines the overall amplitude of the excitation.)

The above parameters can be coded adequately using 6 bits for the pitch, 1 bit for voiced/unvoiced speech, and 5 bits for the gain distributed on a logarithmic scale.

In conclusion, the overal methodology for any form of linear prediction is based on an idealised model. This means that various assumptions are made which are only true in certain ideal conditions. The limitations are therefore apparent in any system that is based on the L.P.C. model. However, the major advantage of the L.P.C. approach is its low overall bit rate for transmission or storage; this, typically, lies between 2400 and 7200 bits per second, depending on the sampling rate used.

4

Speech recognition

4.1 INTRODUCTION

The process of extracting the information content from the spoken word is a formidable task from the point of view of the computer and borders on the area of artificial intelligence. There are several major problem areas in speech recognition (Yannakoudakis, 1985):

(a) Continuous speech has to be segmented in order to obtain the correct information.
(b) Speech patterns vary not only between speakers but also within an individual speaker, even when identical words are spoken.
(c) A word can vary in loudness, pitch, stress and pronunciation rate.
(d) The geographical origin of the speaker is also an important factor when words are pronounced.
(e) Different words can sound very similar.
(f) Background noise and other interference can distort the original signal.
(g) Individual elements tend to lose their identity in the speech process; for example, words merge into each other and phonemes suffer from co-articulation effects.

Because the above problems cover wide areas, research has mostly concentrated on solving specific tasks, such as speaker-dependent recognition and isolated word recognition (Vaissiere, 1985).

There have been two major drives at speech recognition, the simplest one being 'speaker-dependent isolated word recognition' (Rabiner and Levinson, 1981) and the other being 'speaker-independent isolated word recognition' (Atal, 1976; Rosenberg, 1973). Isolated word recognition nicely sidesteps the problem of correctly segmenting continuous speech, by demanding that appropriate pauses are inserted between each word spoken. Speaker-dependent recognition, on the other hand, helps to overcome such problems as regional accent, the sex of the speaker, etc.

Speaker-independent recognition involves converting the spoken word into an electrical signal of some sort via a microphone. The signal is then processed further to obtain a set of identifying features which are then compared with those held in the computer's vocabulary. The vocabulary will consist of a set of reference templates, which have been chosen to represent the average speaker, or speakers with similar accents. Dynamic speaker adaptation is also a viable means for effective speech recognition (Lowerre, 1977). However, the vocabulary size (i.e. number of recognisable words/ utterances) in speaker-independent recognition systems is much smaller than in speaker-dependent systems.

Speaker-dependent isolated word recognition involves training the computer to recognise words by getting the speaker repeatedly to say certain words. From the results of the initial training the computer is able to formulate an average template for individual words, which are then used for reference. Obviously, the more training a machine receives, the better it becomes at choosing the right word(s). Each word must be spoken separately, as opposed to continuously, which is the case in normal speech. The problem here is that the user may not always be prepared to help the machine in this way, since the process can be very time-consuming.

In both cases (speaker-dependent and speaker-independent recognition) some degree of pattern matching is necessary in order to recognise a word. The system compares the incoming signal with a stored template, thereby generating some sort of score on the basis of the degree of similarity. The template with the highest score is then chosen.

The problems which arise with both speaker-dependent and speaker-independent systems are that words will not be pronounced at the same rate by all speakers. This leads to a non-linear distortion of the incoming template compared to the stored template. Consequently, some sort of algorithm is needed to match the incoming template with the stored template, either by shortening or lengthening them accordingly. One such mathematical method is known as 'Dynamic Time Warping' (D.T.W.), where the incoming template is warped in order to align it with the stored template; a score is obtained, on the basis of which the best alternative (template) is then selected (Sakoe and Chiba, 1978; Myers and Levinson, 1982). By applying various grammatical rules the number of templates tested can be reduced significantly, with a consequent reduction in processing time. An alternative approach, adopted by low-cost systems, is to alter both incoming and stored templates to fit a standard length.

Many of the tasks required for voice recognition systems can be handled adequately by isolated word recognition, but continuous speech recognition is much faster and more satisfying to the user, since this is the most natural and efficient way of communication. However, continuous speech recognition systems are much more difficult to implement than isolated word recognition systems. In the former case, the incoming sound wave is usually segmented into small units such as phonemes, diphones, syllables, etc.; the words are then synthesised from these units.

4.2 BASIC STEPS OF SPEECH RECOGNITION

The following are the basic steps required for any speech recognition system, as outlined in Fig. 4.1:

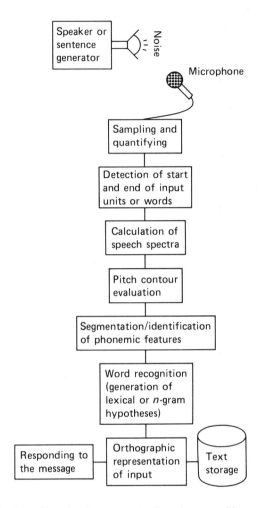

Fig. 4.1 — Functional components of a voice recognition system.

(1)   Sampling
(2)   Detection of start and end of incoming signal
(3)   Calculation of speech spectra, directly from digitisation, or indirectly through filters
(4)   Pitch contour evaluation
(5)   Segmentation
(6)   Word detection, either by applying 'bottom-up' techniques to associate phonemic features with the required lexicon, or 'top-down' techniques in order to identify complete units within the template database
(7)   Responding to a message.

4.2.1 Sampling

Most researchers in speech recognition choose digital techniques over analogue ones because of the accuracy and large storage capability available at the present time.

The speech signal is first sampled and then digitised using an analogue to digital converter. The results from this stage are then stored in the computer. Having obtained the digital representation of the incoming speech signal, various parametric features can then be obtained. These parametric features then form the basis for the segmentation of the speech signal. Techniques for digitising speech signals are discussed in Chapter 3.

Further, to avoid distortion of the incoming signal by background noise, it is desirable to have the microphone as close as possible to the speaker, if it is not possible to operate in a noise-free environment.

4.2.2 Detection of start and end of incoming signal

The signal processor remains in a 'waiting' state when no voice signals high enough to be detected are coming through the receiver (i.e. microphone). A variation in this silent environment is automatically detected by the program in execution and the speech recognition process is activated.

A similar principle applies when the end of an incoming signal is detected, that is, when there is a variation from a signal to silence, and the signal is not of sufficient strength to energise the filters, the speech recognition program recognises this as the end of the utterance.

The algorithms for digitising speech signals also incorporate the necessary logic to detect the start and end of incoming signals by recognising, in effect, the level and variations that occur in the energy source (e.g. from low to high, or from high to low).

4.2.3 Calculation of speech spectra

The performance of this step, together with segmentation (step 5), is critically important to the success of the speech recognition as a whole, because errors made here propagate themselves through the other steps, with disastrous effects on the recognition process. Errors made at the signal processing stage are particularly difficult to recover from, since the information can be lost forever.

Word recognition systems can adopt a number of strategies to identify and extract spectral information, while at the same time minimising the processing time and the storage space necessary for the reference templates. A balance needs to be struck between processing costs and the quality of speech.

It has been demonstrated that the speech signal is more readily understood and its identifying features are more readily extracted when the amplitude of a signal is examined as a function of the frequency (frequency domain). The frequency domain representation of the speech signal provides more information about the articulatory positions and the sound types produced than analysis in the time domain. This is because each type of speech element has certain characteristics — a fact that can readily be demonstrated on the sound spectrograph.

A sound spectrograph utilises a special frequency analyser to produce a three-dimensional plot of the variation in the speech energy spectrum with time. Fig. 4.2 shows a typical example of a sound spectrum (Bristow, 1984).

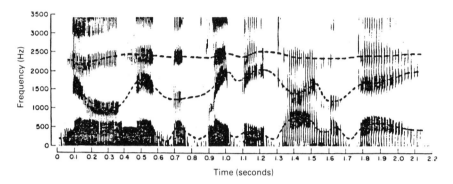

Time (seconds)

'Noon is the sleepy time of day'

Fig. 4.2 — Sound spectrogram of a sentence showing the time variation of the first three vocal resonances, or formants of the first three vocal resonances, or formants. (From G. Bristow: *Electronic Speech Synthesis*, Granada, 1984).

The frequency is given on the vertical axis and time is plotted on the horizontal axis. The energy is denoted by the intensity of the plot: the higher the energy the darker will be the resulting portion of the spectrum. The fine vertical striations in the spectrogram correspond to individual vibrations of the vocal cords. The striations themselves are of differing duration, and these differences arise from the variations of pitch. Thus, the changes in pitch (i.e. the intonation) can be tracked through the spectrogram.

Several dark bands can be seen on the spectrogram, corresponding to the lower few formants which are produced during vowel production. For example, non-nasalised vowels give rise to spectral peaks in the spectrum. These peaks can reliably be correlated to the resonant frequency of the vocal tract at the time of production. Further, the location of a point of constriction in the vocal tract during a plosive release can be indicated by the frequency location of the major energy concentration associated with it.

4.2.4 Pitch contour evaluation
The fundamental frequency of voicing is of use for determining stress and intonation. The contours of the fundamental frequency (as it rises and falls) can also be used as an indication of major syntactic boundaries. Additionally, stress patterns, rhythm and intonation carry some clues as to the phonetic identity of some speech sounds.

4.2.5   Segmentation/Identification of phonemic features

As is the case in step 3, errors made here propagate themselves through the other steps with undesirable effects on the recognition process. It is therefore of vital importance to segment the speech signal correctly. Segmentation can be done either on the basis of some form of phonetic analysis, or according to certain parameters (e.g. voiced/unvoiced). Alternatively, the signal can be segmented in such a way as to ignore anything known about speech by segmenting the signal purely on the basis of time.

4.2.5.1   Segmentation on a time basis

It is possible to analyse the speech signal by chopping it into time segments without making any assumptions as to the duration of phones, phonemes, syllables, etc. It is also possible to ignore the fact that vowels produce formants. In such systems all signals are treated with equal significance, without taking into consideration the fact that some signal differences may be more important than others. The obvious drawback of this approach is the large amount of storage space required. In addition, several different templates may have to be stored for each word in order to take into account the differences which are a direct result of the varying speech rates of individual speakers (Miller, 1981), the channel noise, etc. Thus, some form of speech processing is desirable to eliminate redundant information.

Some of the techniques to eliminate redundant information include:

(a)   Warping the incoming signal to match certain features of the stored templates. For example, the word can be chopped up into segments, each being processed in the normal way. The individual segments for each unit can then be compared with the corresponding units in the stored template. Each segment will be compressed/stretched, as appropriate, until it matches. The amount of distortion required for each segment is then recorded. Finally, the template requiring the least distortion will be selected.

(b)   Detecting certain features of the incoming signal, so that they can be used to adjust the signal to a closer match with the stored template. For example, the fundamental frequency of the incoming signal can be determined and the difference this makes to the stored template can be taken into account. Therefore, irrelevant differences between the stored template and the incoming signal can be reduced.

I.B.M. have built a speech recognition system that uses segmentation on a time basis and is capable of storing and recognising approximately 5000 words. The machine is tuned to the characteristics of each speaker, who initially trains the machine for a period of approximately 20 minutes. The device analyses sounds in segments, each lasting 10 milliseconds. The segments are then compared to a set of 200 basic sound units derived by analysing many sentences. Each word stored in the database is made up of a sequence of these basic sounds. The system does, however, require the speaker to pause between words and it has a success rate of 96.6%.

4.2.5.2 Segmentation according to various parameters

There are a number of parameters available to characterise different speech sounds. These parameters can then be utilised for phonetic processing, that is, to determine the point where the speech signal is to be segmented. A brief summary of some of these parameters (though by no means all) follows:

(1) The fundamental frequency of voiced sounds can be used as an indicator of the presence of voicing (i.e. vowels and sonorants can be determined). However, there are certain limitations to the use of voiced/unvoiced criteria as a means of segmentation. Voiced consonants, for example, tend to be de-voiced in certain environments. Therefore, most recognition systems extract the fundamental frequency of voicing but rarely use it for segmentation purposes. However, the fundamental frequency of voiced sounds can be used to determine the pitch contour; that is, the intonation pattern and stress indicator which can be of vital importance, not only from the point of view of determining major syntactic boundaries, but also if some form of speech understanding is to be incorporated into the system.

(2) One of the most important features of the speech signal arises from the fact that there are sharp variations in the intensity of the signal as a function of time. These sharp variations often indicate changing speech sounds. For example, a low overall intensity would signify a pause, a stop closure, or a weak fricative. All these parameters are related to the energy present in the signal and are obtained by filtering the signal.

(3) It has been shown that the first three formants for vowels and sonorants carry important information about the position of the articulatory organs at the time of production of the speech sounds. These factors can be used to classify vowels and sonorants and, in addition, formant trajectories can be used for diphthong classification.

(4) The gross spectral shape has itself been found useful in the characterisation of some speech sounds, as is the case with the identification of the presence of a fricative, or the onset of plosive releases.

(5) The zero-crossing density can also be used as the basis for segmentation. It is, however, very difficult to associate zero-crossing density with the underlying speech process, because it is not easy to identify speech sounds. Although abrupt changes are encountered in the acoustic signal when (a) nasalisation occurs, (b) there is a sonorant and a fricative sound, (c) there are voiced and unvoiced sections, the boundaries between different states are not always particularly distinct.

4.2.5.3 Segmentation on a phonetic basis

Segmentation can take place at the level of allophone, phoneme, diphone, syllable or word. Each of these is discussed briefly below.

Allophone
Certain allophones can provide word or syllable boundary information which can be very useful in recognition systems. For example, some allophonic variations occur only at the end or beginning of words/syllables. In addition, segmentation at the allophonic level eliminates the need for applying co-articulation rules at a lower level. The disadvantages are that there are many thousands of allophones for any given language, depending on how narrow the phonetic transcription is. Furthermore, the successful identification of the allophone is very much dependent on the context.

Phoneme
The phoneme represents the smallest number of distinctive phonological classes for recognition and is substantially less than the number of allophones, syllables, words, etc. (there are approximately 43 phonemes in the English language). Although the number of phonemes is small, their automatic recognition by a computer system is still a major problem, since there are no acoustically well-defined patterns or templates for phonemes. In addition, each phoneme has a different duration, and certain vowel sounds can be equally assigned to different phonemes, such as the sound [y] in 'pity' and 'city', which can belong to more than one phoneme; these multiple choices demand that more work be carried out at the recognition stage (Zue, 1985). Another problem is that if phonemes are used as the basis for recognition, then more rules will be required at the acoustic level, as well as at the point where the phonemes are turned into words.

Phonetic recognition by the computer has only met with a limited degree of success, achieving recognition rates of approximately 60%. Recognition experiments carried out with trained spectrograph readers had success rates between 85% and 97%, with consonants being identified more reliably than vowels. The experiments demonstrated that the rules used by the experts relied heavily on their own knowledge of contextual influences (Zue and Cole, 1979). This indicates that their expertise is potentially transferable to a computer and that high-performance phonetic recognition is possible.

The phoneme patterns of a language are limited not only by the set of sounds themselves but also by the allowable combinations. These phonotactic constraints are presumably very useful to the native speaker when 'filling in' phonetic details which are either missing or have become distorted. By incorporating rules based on phonotactic constraints into a phonetic recogniser it is believed that more robust speech recognition front-ends can be built.

Diphone
The term diphone is used to represent a vowel–consonant sequence, such that the segment is taken from the centre of the vowel to the centre of the consonant; the segment is often referred to as a 'transeme'. The diphone is employed because a great deal of acoustic information that is used to

identify the consonants lies in the transitions between the consonants and the vowels.

One of the advantages of considering the diphone is that it includes transitional information which is necessary for recognition in many cases. Furthermore, since it is taken across two sounds, it contains within itself some of the co-articulation information which is not present in other units such as the phoneme.

One of the disadvantages with diphones is the large number of diphones (running into thousands). Furthermore, the phonological rules as they are written at present are not easily applied to diphones.

Syllable

Generally speaking, a syllable consists of a vowel and its neighbouring consonants. The theoretical basis for deciding just how to segment a word into its component syllables has yet to be fully agreed by linguists. The advantages are that the nuclei of syllables are relatively easy to locate and identify acoustically. Consequently, they can also form the basis for continuous speech recognition (Hunt, *et al.*, 1980; Ruske and Schotola, 1978; Fujimura, 1975).

The stressed vowels of speech were one of the first groups of sounds to be recognised. As for the diphone, many of the co-articulation effects are contained within the syllable. One of the major disadvantages is the difficulty experienced in determining effectively all syllable boundaries, even though the type and number of syllables present may be known. Again, as is the case for diphones, the number of syllables can become very large, though smaller than that for words and allophones.

Word

Although we as humans can claim to have a good understanding of just what a word is, its acoustic form is very difficult to define. This difficulty arises because when we speak we have a tendency to blend one word into the next. This forms a sort of hybrid word which is neither the first nor the second, but could be construed as a separate entity.

The greatest advantage of dealing with the recognition problem at the word level is that it eliminates the necessity for sometimes complex algorithms to match phonemes, allophones, etc., with the stored words. By going directly from the input to the template for the stored word, much time can be saved. The main disadvantages are that when dealing with a very large lexicon (Shipman and Zue, 1982), the scanning of the templates to find the best match can be very time-consuming. There are many algorithms to reduce the number of templates scanned; an example here is the use of partial phonetic information in lexical (word) access (Huttenlocher, and Zue 1984). There is also the problem of recognising word boundaries, because when we speak we tend to anticipate the next word. This results in the beginnings, and in particular the ends, of words being distorted from the stored templates of words spoken in isolation. The problem then becomes one of determining how a template may be distorted in these situations.

4.2.6 Word recognition

If segmentation takes place at a level lower than a word, some means of getting from the lower level to that of stored words has to be included in the system (Levinson, 1984). There is a certain degree of uncertainty when trying to assign words to segmented data, and in many cases it is possible to assign more than one word to the data (De Mori, 1983). When this occurs, an algorithm has to be included in the system which can generate the most likely word. The algorithm may include some form of syntactical analysis in order to weed out ungrammatical sequences, as well as some knowledge of the most likely words in a particular context. Thus, some knowledge of the semantics and pragmatics of a language can be incorporated into a speech recognition system. This can, however, make the recognition system very task-specific.

If the speech signal is viewed as a composite pattern in which a relatively few primitive patterns are combined in a multi-level hierarchy (e.g. bit, segment, word, etc.) then the patterns can be combined probabilistically and deterministically to form strings at the semantic level (Levinson, 1984).

Syntactical analysis can also be used to restrict the recognition of the next word on the basis of previously stored words. This is desirable, because with large lexicons the task of searching for the best match can become very expensive computationally. However, due to the vagaries of the English language, this syntactical approach has certain limitations, including the difficulty in distinguishing between well-formed and poorly formed sentences.

A statistical approach can be adopted at all levels of decision making (Jelineck, 1976; Jelineck et al., 1983) where a score can be assigned to each of the alternatives on the basis of past history; the alternative with the highest score being the one selected for further processing. There are many ways of obtaining the highest score. The 'breadth first search' computes the score at each alternative and selects the route with the highest score. The 'depth first search' selects the highest score at the initial level and then pursues this initial choice in subsequent levels, in a 'depth first' manner. The problem with the 'depth first' technique is that the system is committed to the consequences of the first choice. There are also searching techniques which are a hybrid of 'breadth first' and 'depth first' techniques.

4.2.7 Responding to the message

Assuming that all the words and sentences have been correctly identified, the computer must then be able to respond in the appropriate manner. The response can be in the form of an execution of an operating system command, the display of a string (message) on the screen, the lexical display of the words actually spoken, etc. However, we must point out here that, at this step and beyond, the response is related to the degree of 'intelligence' built into the computer system as a whole.

4.3 CONCLUSIONS

Systems which have the components dicsussed in this chapter can be structured in many ways, and the approach which has been outlined so far is termed 'bottom-up'. Important acoustic parameters are first extracted (signal processing), followed by phonetic assignment, then word matching with lexical entries, then syntactic, semantic and pragmatic analysis. Generally speaking, the technique starts with the small units, and gradually works up to the larger ones at higher conceptual levels.

An alternative approach is the 'top-down', where we start by predicting sentences, hypothesising phrases, words, stress, intonation, phonemes, etc., and then compare the input with the hypothesised form. Some systems in fact utilise both top-down and bottom-up techniques, using one to reinforce the other.

The emphasis in speech recognition has been on pattern matching of word-sized units with those already stored on the database. The limited storage, the problems associated with finding the best match, and insufficient speed for digital processing, have all hindered progress in this area. In the near future, parallel processors and intelligent algorithms that utilise parallel architectures fully will clearly help to resolve these problems.

We believe that the only way forward is to design algorithms which identify the phonetic components of incoming signals and proceed to use these to synthesise words by means of phoneme-to-n-gram mappings; an n-gram is a string of n consecutive letters that occur naturally in words/sentences. A carefully chosen table of n-grams and corresponding sounds/phonemes can then be used as the basis for phoneme-to-n-gram and n-gram-to-word transformations. The synthesised words can then be transferred to another module, such as a spelling detector and corrector (Yannakoudakis, 1983), for further evaluation.

Most of the current speech recognition systems are based on the spectral representation of the speech signal. This representation is very useful for analysis and synthesis where the goal is natural-sounding speech, but there is no reason to believe that what is good for synthesis is good for recognition. After all, the two tasks are very different.

As mentioned in Chapter 1, the sound received at the eighth cranial nerve has passed through the human auditory system and as such it is not a close copy of the sound originally produced by the speaker. Therefore, it will not be the same when examined spectrographically.

The ear acts as a filter on the incoming signal; for example, we know that low-frequency signal analysis is significantly better than high-frequency analysis. This is of particular significance when analysing sonorants, which are determined better using low frequencies.

Designers of speech recognition systems have started experimenting with systems that are capable, in a limited sense, of mimicking the human auditory process, and in particular the filtering action of the ear (Klatt, 1982). It is expected that irrelevant acoustic variabilities will be reduced and that the phonetic contrasts will be enhanced.

5

Speech synthesis

5.1 INTRODUCTION

There are two aspects to speech synthesis. The first is concerned with determining the stored units (e.g. phonemes, words, sentences, etc.) and the various methods of producing realistic-sounding (smooth) speech. The second is concerned with the hardware required (i.e. the synthesiser). The synthesiser accepts the parameters produced by the synthesis logic, converts these to analogue signals and then produces the required sound.

In this chapter, we are going to discuss the overall speech synthesis process, that is, the characteristics of a system that converts strings (words, sentences, etc.) to sound (Bristow, 1984).

5.2 SPEECH SYNTHESISERS

The main objective of digital coding (in the present context) is to reduce the number of bits per second needed to store the speech signal, and to reproduce an acceptable sound. By reducing the number of bits per second a reduction in cost is achieved, since the fewer the bits, the less memory is required to store the utterances. Unfortunately, low bit rates are usually accompanied by a reduction in the speech quality. A further disadvantage is that, where low bit rates are employed, the actual encoding of the speech can be extremely complex and time-consuming. A balance has to be obtained between the bit rate used and the quality of the resultant speech. What may be desirable in one set of circumstances may not be so in another.

There are two main categories of speech synthesisers available for speech synthesis: those that utilise a 'time domain' technique and those that utilise a 'frequency domain'.

5.2.1 Time domain

The time domain technique entails digitising the whole of the analogue signal. Here, the stored data represent a compressed waveform as a function of time, and the action of the synthesiser is to unpack the data and produce the speech signal.

It is wrong to assume that the goal with time domain synthesis is to approximate the original signal as closely as possible, with the lowest number of bits obtainable. Rather, its aim is to produce a synthetic waveform which may not necessarily bear any visual resemblance to the original signal when looked at spectrographically, but will, however, be perceived by the listener to be the same. The basic idea is to extract only the relevant information from the signal. There have been several developments in this area away from the more conventional digital coding techniques. One such method is the 'Mozer technique' (discussed in Chapter 3), which achieves bit rates as low as 1000 bits per second.

The advantage of using a time domain technique over a frequency domain technique is that the equipment needed is simple; a digital-to-analogue converter and a post-sampling filter are all that is needed if P.C.M. is used. Another advantage is that the speech quality can easily be controlled by selecting a suitable sampling rate and coding scheme. The time domain technique also produces a more natural sound than the frequency domain technique.

5.2.2 Frequency domain

Frequency domain synthesis schemes are based on the modelling of human speech according to whether or not it is voiced or unvoiced, as well as the resonance states of the vocal tract. Data compression is obtained by storing these two parameters separately. Before these parameters can be output, it is necessary to convert them back into a time domain form. This leads to more circuitry being required for the conversion and a more complicated and expensive system.

5.3 SPEECH SYNTHESIS SYSTEMS

The most obvious way to output speech may seem to be to select the appropriate speech units (e.g. sentences, words, syllables, phonemes) and then to record these units digitally. These units can then be concatenated to form the desired utterances. The units can be stored on a disk, and in fact the technology now exists to store up to one working month of continuous speech by using some form of linear predictive coding. The only problem in this case would be the actual time it would take to record the utterances. In the following section we discuss some possible units and their relative merits.

5.3.1 Unit size
5.3.1.1 Words
If the word is chosen as the basic unit, as might seem the sensible choice, there are two problem areas which soon become apparent, depending on the synthesiser being used.

If the words have been recorded as time waveforms of the individual words, the inclusion of intonation, co-articulation, etc., can become extremely difficult, if not impossible, using conventional time domain techniques such as P.C.M. If the prosodic features are not included, then the concatenated speech can sound very false because of the lack of appropriate stress and intonation. In addition, the words would not be co-articulated properly, since words said in isolation do not sound the same as words said during the process of continuous speech. The prosodic features (e.g. pitch, intonation) affect not only individual words but stretch across whole sentences.

If on the other hand, the words have been coded in frequency domain, the essential features of word-to-word co-articulation, rhythm and intonation can be incorporated. The resulting speech can sound very synthetic, because natural speech is not always pure voiced or pure unvoiced but a blend of both.

The major problem with using words to synthesise speech is the large vocabulary needed for unrestricted speech synthesis. It is, however, one of the most widely used approaches for synthesis, because the algorithm is easy to implement and does not require many rules.

5.3.1.2 Sentences

One simple way of overcoming the lack of appropriate prosodic and other features might seem to be to record whole sentences/phrases, and string them together as required. The disadvantages are of course the very heavy demand this can make on storage, memory, etc., and hence sentences/phrases are of use only in situations where a limited lexicon is required. One method for limiting the storage requirements is to insert words in the appropriate place in the sentence, as in the following example where the units stored are 'Please deposit', 'pounds', 'ten', 'twenty' and 'thirty':

> Please deposit...pounds.
> (ten)
> (twenty)
> (thirty)

Difficulties occur when the same word needs to be inserted in several different places, because what sounds right in one context does not necessarily sound right in another. The problem here is the incorrect placement of stress and intonation, as well as co-articulation. For example, the TEN in 'Please deposit TEN pounds', and the TEN in 'Your flight leaves at TEN thirty' must be recorded separately under each context and then edited and stored individually. This methodology is, however, acceptable in certain circumstances, such as when a limited vocabulary is used.

5.3.1.3 Morphemes

The English language consists of approximately 300 000 words, although this does not include borrowed or foreign words which can also be found in unrestricted text. For general applications of speech synthesis from unrestricted text (Allen *et al.*, 1979; Elovitz *et al.*, 1976), the limitations of synthesis from words and sentences soon become obvious.

One level down from a word as a unit, might be to store the base of a word plus all the various endings; for example, the following might be stored:

look

ed

cook

s

From this, it would be possible to generate the words 'look', 'looks', 'looked', 'cook', 'cooks', 'cooked'. However, the dictionary required may still be prohibitively large for speech from unrestricted text.

Alternative storage units are the morphemes of the language. The English language contains approximately 12 000 morphemes and these can be stored in the vocabulary of the system without too many overheads.

If we decide to store the 'utterances' at a level below that of the word, such as a morpheme, some sort of methodology becomes necessary for breaking the words for synthesis down into the correct units (if the aim is to synthesise words from unrestricted text). The alternative is for the input into the system to be entered by hand, in a form that is acceptable to the machine. In this case, the morphemes of the words would have to be entered. An algorithm also needs to be included to concatenate the stored fragments into words. This algorithm will generally have to perform some sort of blending process, otherwise the speech will be of poor quality. The stored templates need to be blended together; this process is known as 'interpolation'.

5.3.1.4 Syllables
If the syllable is stored as the basic unit (Radhakrishnan and Castillo, 1981), then we have to use some form of source filter representation. This is because, although it is necessary to have co-articulation between different words to make the resultant speech sound fluent, co-articulation is also required between syllables to make the resultant speech comprehensible. Therefore, it becomes necessary to use a source filter model.

There is considerable practical difficulty in obtaining syllables ready for storage. It lies not so much in the recording of the syllables but in the editing, where cuts have to be made in exactly the right place so that the resultant speech does not sound strange. The smaller the units that are chosen, the more sensitive the editing job becomes. This is an unenviable task considering that there are approximately 10 000 syllables in the English language.

5.3.1.5 Phonemes and allophones
Another approach to synthesise unrestricted speech involves the use of phonemes. Since there are only approximately 43 phonemes in the English language, the vocabulary does not need to be large and the input to the system can be a phonetic transcription of the desired speech.

However, the problem here is determining what to store. The phoneme is not a concrete entity but rather a logical representation of a group of speech sounds (allophones). It is estimated that there are between 120 and 1000 allophones in the English language, depending on how detailed the phonetic transcription is.

For speech synthesis there are rules/algorithms available to convert a word into its allophonic components. In practice, only approximately 200 allophonic variations are used (O'Shaughnessy, 1983). Clearly, the more details (rules) are incorporated in this transformation, the better the quality of speech, whilst at the same time the prosodic features of the language will be represented more effectively.

If the speech synthesis algorithm does not operate on rules then the input to the system needs to be an allophonic transcription. This requires a large amount of skill and patience on the part of the person making the transcription in order to produce reasonable-sounding speech.

Interpolation becomes neccesary because the vocal tract does not change shape abruptly. Tongue, lips and teeth are in constant motion, gliding smoothly from one articulatory position to the next. This makes it is virtually impossible to determine where an allophone stops and another begins. Analysis of frequency spectra has demonstrated that the transitions are between sets of 'target' configurations, as opposed to the 'actual' configurations. To overcome this problem, we need to incorporate the effect of the transitions into their smoothing algorithms by inserting interpolated sets of parameters between neighbouring phonemes. This approach works reasonably well for slow transitions, as is the case with vowels, but not with relatively fast transitions, such as those occurring between consonants where important acoustic cues can be missed. One way to overcome this is to use diphones or demisyllables.

5.3.1.6 Demisyllables and Diphones
The sound segments which comprise the transition from the centre of one phone to the centre of the next are known as diphones. The aim here is the use of demisyllables or diphones as the units for concatenation (Fujimura et al., 1977).

If diphones are used, the input is a phonetic transcription which relates to a synthetic lexicon. This ensures that discontinuities do not arise between segments beginning and ending with the same phoneme. Consequently, interpolation becomes irrelevant.

Strictly speaking, diphones are not demisyllables, although the two are very similar. For example, in the simplest case, two diphones characterise a syllable comprising the sequence: consonant–vowel–consonant. A demisyllable therefore comprises the sequence: consonant–vowel or vowel–consonant.

There is an advantage in using demisyllables as opposed to diphones as the basic units, because many syllables end with complicated consonant clusters which are difficult to produce convincingly with diphone concatenation. There are between 1000 and 2000 diphones/demisyllables compared to between 4000 to 10000 syllables.

It has been shown that the rhythm of speech affects the duration of the syllable in different situations. The effects here appear to be concentrated on the duration of the vowel and the closing consonant cluster, as opposed to the initial consonant cluster. Therefore, demisyllables can be used effectively to deal with rhythm. In addition, demisyllables provide the means for some form of differential lengthening to be applied at the appropriate place.

What we have been discussing can be referred to as 'synthesis by concatenating pre-stored units'. This is generally characterised by the large amount of stored data that is required where unrestricted speech is to be produced.

Another method for unrestricted speech synthesis is known as 'synthesis by rule'. It involves two separate stages. In the first stage a sequence of characters (e.g. a word or a sentence) is accepted, the phonetic components (e.g. phonemes, allophones, syllables) are identified and syntactic information is then extracted. The result of this stage is a string of symbols representing the sound units, pauses, boundaries between words, phrases and sentences. In the second stage the symbols are matched with the stored units, they are linked, and the resulting coded waveform is then sent to an output device for decoding (e.g. the synthesiser).

The reason the above process is called 'synthesis by rule' is because rules are used to govern the transitions between the various speech segments. For example, rules are available to convert phonemes to allophones. The construction of rules requires extensive knowledge and deep understanding of speech production and perception processes at work in a language. The rules must take into account all the perceptually different realisations that the phonetic segments undergo in different environments. There are usually exceptions to most rules and these have to be incorporated either within the rules, or in an exception table which has to be examined first.

Clearly, synthesis by rule is more viable for producing speech from unrestricted text than synthesis from concatenation of pre-recorded units. This is because the number of units stored is considerably less in synthesis by rule than in synthesis by concatenation.

5.4   A GENERAL EXAMPLE OF SYNTHESIS BY RULE

Fig. 5.1 represents the functional components of a text-to-speech system, starting with the actual storage and organisation of the rules, their utilisation and finally the activation of the voice synthesiser. The logic presented here can be applied to all text-to-speech systems where the text is unrestricted and therefore any given English word can be decomposed into its equivalent phonetic features (Elovitz *et al.*, 1976).

Speech synthesis systems which aim to produce speech from unrestricted text must first perform some sort of normalisation of the text. The system must cope with abbreviations, punctuation marks, capital letters, numbers, etc. In other words, it should produce normalised output; for example, 'Mr Emmanuel' should be converted to 'Mister Emmanuel' and then synthesised accordingly.

Some form of syntax analysis and sentence parsing is also desirable in order to be able to include appropriate rhythm, intonation, pitch, stress, etc. These factors can operate at the sentence/phrase level as well as at the word

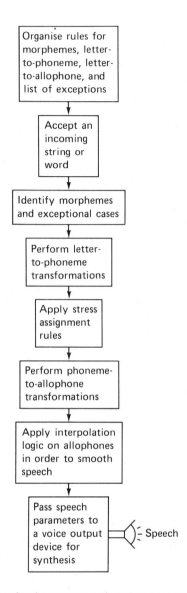

Fig. 5.1 — Functional components of a text-to-speech system.

level. The results from this form of analysis would then be included in the output.

The string 'matching strings' is used to demonstrate the process of word decomposition and synthesis by rule. The first stage might be to insert appropriate markers to indicate a pause. If, for example, the symbol * replaced a space and therefore represented a pause, and the symbol ** an extended pause, then the result of the first phase would be

matching*strings**

The morpheme stripper would then be able to generate the correct morphemes from the incoming text. A morpheme stripper may be included because the rules which are used to convert letters to phonemes do not always apply across morpheme boundaries. Examples of these cases are the words 'changeable', 'tear', 'reach', 'streak', where 'ea' has different pronunciations, and the words 'mischance' and 'school', where the consonants 'sch' are split between morpheme boundaries.

Morpheme stripping is achieved by utilising a set of rules that define the morphemes to be extracted in a given set of circumstances. Since the English language cannot be completely defined by a set of rules, a list of exceptions is also required. The list of exceptions can include words with an apostrophe (e.g. they're, I'll), commonly occurring foreign or specialised words, etc. Thus, the morpheme-stripping algorithm must search the list of exceptions first and if no match is found the more general rules are then applied.

It has been demonstrated that by applying a morpheme-stripping function, before applying letter-to-phoneme rules, better speech quality is obtained than with the alternative method of applying the letter-to-phoneme rules directly to the words themselves. The disadvantages here are that more rules are required as well as a larger lexicon. The alternative to the morphene-stripping function would be to have a large dictionary of exceptions for word-to-phoneme transformations.

Returning to the example 'matching strings': The second phase would be the application of the rules to break the words down into the appropriate morphemes, firstly by checking the exceptions and then by applying the more general rules. If the symbol '+' is used to represent a morpheme boundary, the result of the second phase would be:

match+ing*string+s**

Some problems may arise because it is impossible to detect every morpheme boundary by using rules, and the program will inevitably make mistakes unless it utilises a large dictionary of exceptions. Rules also need to be applied at the concatenation phase, that is, when the various segments are being joined together for synthesis.

Having extracted the morphemes, the letter-to-phoneme rules can be applied. Our string thus becomes:

/m//ae//t//ch//+//ih//nx//*//s//t//r//in//nx//+//z//**/

It is at this stage that indicators regarding suprasegmental features, particularly pitch and intonation, are used to enrich the string further. Once the letter-to-phoneme transformations have taken place, the rules for stress assignment within the units can be applied. Allophonic variations in English vowels are determined by syllabic stress as well as by neighbouring phones. Consequently, the rules for stress assignment need to be applied before the rules for phoneme-to-allophone.

Finally, the rules for the conversion of the phonemes to allophones are applied. At this stage, the results are ready to be passed to a speech synthesiser. The results from the phoneme-to-allophone conversion are often a set of parameters which can be directly understood by the speech synthesiser. Before the results are sent for synthesis, some form of interpolation logic may need to be applied so that the transitions from one allophone to the next are perceived as being relatively smooth.

5.5 CONCLUSIONS

Although synthesis by rule is relatively simple and attractive at the implementation stage, the resulting speech can often sound mechanical. This can be acceptable in some circumstances although not in others. To a certain extent, this can be overcome if systems are developed to generate more phonetic detail, particularly at the allophonic level.

The prosodic features of a language are particularly important for understanding the information conveyed, and for the listener to interpret correctly the message conveyed. It has been demonstrated that when speech is monotonous (i.e. when stress, rhythm, and intonation are not included), the listener finds it very difficult to maintain interest in the conversation.

6

A voice output language

6.1 INTRODUCTION

In this chapter, we are going to discuss a voice output language which consists of simple control codes that activate a speech synthesiser. Our ultimate objective is to demonstrate that speech synthesis (i.e. the conversion of text to speech) can be performed by simple and effective codes, as far as the user is concerned; the complexity behind such a conversion is of no inherent interest to the user. For a deeper understanding of the rules whereby text is converted to speech, the reader can study the program we present in Appendix A.

Rather than discuss possible voice output commands hypothetically, we choose to describe a well-tested system, that is currently on offer by INFOVOX. This is the SA 201/PC system which we have used extensively at the University of Bradford. It comes in the form of a single card with language-dependent software (e.g. English, French, German) provided separately (e.g. on floppy disk). All the user has to do is load the software onto the memory of the card and assume he has an extra peripheral upon which text can be 'written'. This peripheral is logically named 'speech' and can in fact be assumed to be another printer connected to the computer. The initialisation of the card is carried out by the program INITALK XX where XX denotes the language to be used. For example, INITALK AM loads the American/English rules, and INITALK FR loads the French rules.

The following is an example program, written in the language Pascal, that accepts one sentence after the other and transfers it to the peripheral SPEECH; the full stop, by default, activates the actual production of speech, while the word 'STOP' terminates the execution of this program:

```
program speak(Input, Output, Speech);
    type A string = STRING[250];
var
    Speech: TEXT;
    InputString: Astring;
    Continue: BOOLEAN;
begin
    Continue := True; Assign(Speech, 'Speech'); rewrite(Speech);
```

```
        while Continue
            do begin
                writeln(Output, 'Please type a line (STOP to exit)');
                readln(Input, InputString);
                if InputString = 'STOP'
                    then Continue := False
                    else writeln(Speech, InputString)
            end
    end.
```

The software of the SA 201/PC system is downloaded from the disk memory to the expansion card. The software for text-to-speech conversion is based on the principles outlined in Fig. 6.1.

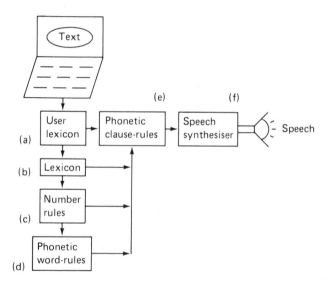

Fig. 6.1 — Outline of a text-to-speech system.

The basic function of the software is to convert arbitrary texts to control parameters to the speech synthesiser circuit. The texts can be either normally spelled texts (orthographic texts) or special phonetic texts. The conversion is carried out in a number of steps as follows:

(a)   The text written to the SA 201/PC is first searched for in a user lexicon. This lexicon can be accessed by the user himself for entry of frequently used abbreviations and words (e.g. foreign names) that might be pronounced in a wrong way when using the text-to-speech rules of the system. If the word is found in the user lexicon, it will be replaced by the text or phonetic code given by the lexicon. The lexicon search is recursive, that is, the text replacing the look-up word might in itself contain words that could be found as another look-up word in the lexicon.

(b) The text word is then searched for in a fixed pronunciation lexicon. This lexicon gives the correct pronunciation of the most frequent exceptions to the text-to-speech rules. If the word is found in the fixed lexicon, it will be replaced by a corresponding phonetic code.

(c) If the text contains digits, it will be treated with the system module that defines the pronunciation of digit combinations. The digits '1987' are thus pronounced as 'Nineteenhundredeightyseven'. Observe that the period after a digit is regarded as a decimal point if followed by a digit. The SA 201/PC then waits for one more (non-digit) character after the period before reading the text.

(d) Text that was not treated according to (a)–(c) above is processed with a general rule module for conversion of normal text to phonetic text code. Together with the fixed pronunciation lexicon, this module correctly converts the 10000 most frequent English words (and most other English words as well) to phonetic text.

(e) The phonetic phrase-rules start out from phonetic text code for each word and generate the control parameters for the synthesiser circuit. Examples are rules that adapt the speech sounds to the context (e.g. rules for co-articulation and rules for reduction of sounds). The intonation of the speech (the prosody) is also determined in this part of the system.

(f) The parameters generated by the phonetic phrase-rules control the speech synthesiser circuit. The synthesiser is a model of the human speech production system, built around a special circuit (a signal processor) that has been programmed to produce speech.

The signal processor itself is a stand-alone microprocessor system built around the Motorola MC68000 central processing unit (CPU) with 128 kilobytes of random access memory (RAM) and 16 kilobytes of erasable programmable read only memory (EPROM). The hardware includes a parallel interface to the computer bus and specially programmed signal processor (NEC 7720), which is used as a voice generator. The block diagram of the hardware is presented in Fig. 6.2.

The SA 201/PC communicates with the computer via the parallel interface. Sixteen kilobytes of RAM are used by a language-independent program to control text entry, handling of commands and output of speech parameters to the signal processor. Approximately 70 kilobytes of RAM are used by the language-specific program (i.e. for the text-to-speech conversion).

The signal processor simulates the speech production system by generating voiced and unvoiced sounds to a digital filter network. The filter parameter values are controlled from the microprocessor system. New parameter values are sent to the synthesiser every 10 milliseconds, at normal speech rate.

Computer bus

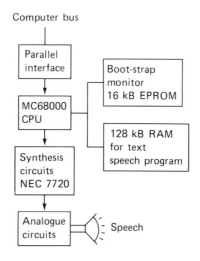

Fig. 6.2 — Block diagram of hardware for text-to-speech.

6.2   VOICE OUTPUT FUNCTIONS

Reading modes

In this section, we present the various codes for speech production and setting of parameters. The letters 'ESC' stand for the escape character; usually decimal number 27 in the ASCII code. Each code is in the form of an escape character, followed by one or more alphanumeric characters, which are 'written' on to the device SPEECH. The actual text is then transferred on to the device in a similar manner and the software of the SA 201/PC automatically converts this to speech.

The SA 201/PC can be controlled to perform the reading in different modes. The system can read the text either letter by letter (letter mode), word by word (word mode), sentence by sentence (sentence mode) or combined word by word and sentence by sentence.

In letter mode, each letter is read as soon as it has been received by the program.

In word mode, the word is read after a space character (or other word delimiter) has been received.

In sentence mode, the program waits for period, exclamation mark or question mark before the sentence is read. The intonation of the sentence is influenced by the punctuation.

When using the combined word/sentence mode, each word is read after a space. The whole sentence is also read as in sentence mode.

Line mode is similar to sentence mode, with the addition that the speech output is also started after carriage return <cr>.

In sentence mode, a certain delay is noticed after the text has been sent to the SA 201/PC and before the speech starts. This is because the rule system has to analyse the text string and the delay might become noticeable when using long sentences. In the 'fast reading mode', the speech output is started in word mode and automatically switched over to sentence mode, when the letter mode 'catches up'. The various codes for the reading mode are as follows:

Change to letter mode	ESC B
Change to letter mode and distinguish between upper and lower case characters	ESC b
Change to word mode	ESC O
Change to sentence mode	ESC R (default)
Change to combined word and sentence mode	ESC K
Change to line mode	ESC R
Change to fast reading mode	ESC A

Type of voice
Four different basic voices can be used. All the voices can be modified with the other codes for speed, variation, aspiration, etc. The codes for selection of basic voice are:

Change to normal male voice	ESC PV1 (default)
Change to light voice	ESC PV2
Change to dark male voice	ESC PV3
Change to very light voice	ESC PV4

When changing the type of voice, all other voice quality parameters are reset to default values.

Speech rate
The speech rate can be varied in steps. A normal speech rate during conversation is approximately 150 words per minute. The codes for selection of speech rate are:

Change to speech rate n
    $n = 1$–9. 1 corresponds to very low rate, 9 corresponds to very high rate. This code gives absolute control of the speech rate in course steps.
    Default: $n = 5$.
	ESC Tn

Increase the speech rate by approximately 12%	ESC T+
Increase the speech rate by approximately 25%	ESC F
Decrease the speech rate by approximately 12%	ESC T−
Decrease the speech rate by approximately 25%	ESC L

Pitch level (fundamental frequency)
The pitch level (fundamental frequency) of the voice can be varied in steps.
The pitch level determines the lightness or darkness of the voice. The codes
for control of the pitch level are:

Change to pitch level n
    $n = 1$–9. 1 corresponds to very low pitch level. 9
    corresponds to very high pitch level. This code
    gives absolute control of the pitch level.
    For the default value see Table 6.1.   ESC Pn
Increase the pitch level one step   ESC P+
Decrease the pitch level one step   ESC P−

Pitch variation
In a sentence, the voice pitch variation creates the so-called prosody of the
sentence. The prosody can be emphasised accordingly (i.e. it can be
increased or decreased). The SA 201/PC can be controlled to different
degrees of pitch variation and the voice will be perceived as more expressive,
less expressive, or monotone. The codes to control the prosody are:

Change to pitch variation level n
    $n = 0$-9. 0 corresponds to a voice with very low
    pitch variation. 9 corresponds to a very dyna-
    mic voice.
    For the default value see Table 6.1   ESC PDn

Aspiration
The aspiration is the unvoiced sound that emanates at the vocal cords, when
for example we are whispering. The SA 201/PC voice can be controlled to
aspirate accordingly. The codes to control aspiration are:

Change to aspiration level n
    $n = 0$–9. 0 corresponds to a voice with very
    little aspiration. 9 corresponds to a whispering
    voice.
    For the default value see Table 6.1   ESC PAn

Table 6.1 — Default values for pitch level, pitch variation and aspiration

Type of voice		Pitch	Pitch variation	Aspiration
Normal male voice	(PV1)	5	3	0
Light voice	(PV2)	8	5	1
Dark male voice	(PV3)	5	4	0
Very light voice	(PV4)	9+	6	2

Loudness
The volume of the speech can be controlled with the potentiometer of the card. The volume can also be controlled with program codes. The codes for loudness control are:

Change to speech with loudness level n
$n = 0$–9. 0 corresponds to silence. 9 corresponds to
normal level. Each step changes the output level by
3 dB. The default value for n is 9.   ESC Gn

Tone codes
In addition to voice production, the system can generate tone signals. The duration, frequency and loudness of the tones can be varied as indicated below:

Generate a tone with frequency x, level y and
duration z ESC #xyz
—x is the frequency of the tone on a 12-tone scale.
  $X = A$–Z.
  $A = 116$ Hz, $Z = 494$ Hz (approximately)
—y is the tone level on a decibel scale.
  $y = A$–Z
  A corresponds to silence. Z is the strongest tone
  level.
—z is the duration of the tone.
  $y = A$–Z.
  A is the unit length. Z corresponds to 26 times the
  unit length.

The tone codes cannot be buffered. Before giving a new tone code, the previous tone has to finish.

Optionally, #xyz can be sent back to the computer as a confirmation that the tone is finished. See also under 'Flags (selectable functions)' below.

Save and retrieve sentences
The SA 201/PC contains nine buffers in which sentences can be saved for later repetition. The codes for storage/retrieval of sentences are:

Save the sentence just spoken in
Buffer number n
$n = 1$–9. A sentence previously saved in the buffer
will be erased.   ESC Un
Read the sentence saved in sentence
Buffer number n
$n = 1$–9. If there is no sentence stored in this buffer,
SA 201/PC will say 'empty'   ESC Vn

The maximum length of a sentence to be saved in the buffers is 64 characters. If longer sentences are saved, they will use the following buffer.

Indexing
It is possible to introduce indexes in the text in order to indicate to the computer the utterance just pronounced by the SA 201/PC. This feature is useful for synchronising the speech with other activities controlled by the computer. The indexes are sent back to the computer when the character followed by the index is pronounced. This can be the first character of the next word or the pause corresponding to a punctuation mark. The codes for indexing are:

Define x as index character   ESC %x
x can be any character with the exception of 'erase'
and '='. Of course, one should not select index
characters that could interfere with normal text or
codes.
Disable the indexing   ESC % <'erase'>
Repeat (to the computer) the last index   ESC %=

Flags (selectable functions)
Some functions of the SA 201/PC are optionally selectable. The codes are:

Switch on the function x ESC =x+
Switch off the function x ESC =x−

If x equals B The system says 'Begin' (or the equivalent in a different language) at restart or when changing language (default = off).

If *x* equals R   The system repeats the last spoken sentence after a 'space' character. No other character can be written between the sentence and the 'space' (default = off).

If *x* equals S   Speech is interrupted in letter mode when typing the next character (default = on).

If *x* equals #   When a tone code has been given and the tone has been terminated, the tone code is sent back to the computer (default = off).

Miscellaneous codes
— General reset code (ESC): Resets all parameters to default values, clears all internal buffers and all saved sentences.
— General reset code (ESC Z): The same function as ESC except that indexing still works the same as before the reset.
— Partial reset code (ESC Z): Clears only the internal buffers for text and speech. Sentences saved with ESC Un are retained.
— Change the code prefix to the ASCII character x (ESC Cx).
— Change the erase key from the character used as 'erase' (normally <backapace>) to the ASCII character x (ESC Dx).
— Stop the speech output (ESC S): This code stops the current output of speech, but the handling of text input continues (until the internal buffers become full). When speech output is resumed (with ESC Q), the system begins to speak from where it stopped. A similar function can be obtained by just writing ESC. The output then stops. Output is resumed when any non-functional code such as 'space' is written. However, in this case the processing of text input does not continue during the pause.
— Resume the speech output (ESC Q): Resume the speech output interrupted by ESC S.
— Suppress speech output of certain text (ESC (<text>ESC): The text between ESC (and ESC) is not converted to speech.

6.3   PHONETIC TEXT

There are two ways of using phonetic text to change the pronunciation. Either normally spelled text can be mixed with phonetically spelled text, or the user's lexicon can be used with phonetic text. In both cases, the phonetic text code has to be enclosed by the character '#'.

6.3.1   Rules for using phonetic text

Below is a list of phonetic input symbols for English text-to-speech conversion. They are quite similar to the 'ARPAbet', a standardised phoneme description symbol set for American English. An example is given with each symbol. Note that all single symbols are upper case and that all double symbols are lower case. Use of non-defined text symbols (such as a double symbol in upper case) may cause the synthesis to stop. Part of the text might then be lost during the reading.

VOWELS

iy	beet	ih	bit
ey	bait	eh	bet
ow	boat	ah	but
uw	boot	uh	book
ae	bat	aa	Bob
ao	bought	er	bird
ay	bite	aw	bout
oy	boy	yu	beauty
ax	about	ix	impart
ar	bar	ir	beer
or	boar	ur	poor

PLOSIVE CONSONANTS

B	ban	p	pan
D	dam	T	tan
G	game	K	can
Q	atevery (American)	dx	butter (American)

FRICATIVE CONSONANTS

V	van	F	fan
dh	than	th	thin
z	zoo	S	so
zh	azure	sh	shore
hh	hat	el	table

AFFRICATIVE CONSONANTS

jh	jet	ch	chin

NASAL CONSONANTS

M	met	n	net
nx	sing		

ORAL CONSONANTS

W	wet	Y	yet
R	right	L	let

STRESS SYMBOLS

The stress symbols are always placed before the stressed vowel in the following manner:

' primary lexicon stress	PR'ayM	(Prime)
	PR'ayMaxRiy	(Primary; single stress)
" secondary lexicon stress	PR'ayM"ehRiy	(Primary; double stress)
	P'ahRM"ihT	(Permit; nominal pronunciation)

The digits 0–9 in front of a word determine the stress of the entire word in a phrase. This feature can be used to give extra stress or less stress to a word in a phrase as follows:

0	Makes the word completely without stress.
1	Gives stress to a word normally without stress.
2	Is the normal rule-determined stress on most words.
3–9	Gives a varying degree of emphatic stress.

These digits are phonetic symbols but can be used in normal text if embraced by '#' signs. For example, compare 'Mary was stronger than I thought' with '#7#'Mary was stronger than I thought'.

6.3.2   Punctuation marks

The following punctuation marks are used as in normal texts:

.	period
,	comma
!	exclamation mark
?	question mark

Punctuation marks influence the intonation and duration of speech utterances. The comma produces a short pause, whereas the rest produce longer pauses, indicating the end of a sentence.

6.4   LEXICON OF THE USER

The user's lexicon is a file with the name XXULEX.IVX. By entering a word in the user's lexicon one can determine the pronunciation of the word. Sometimes the rule system will generate a pronunciation that is not acceptable (e.g. for some foreign names). Sometimes the pronunciation of an abbreviation is wanted in the non-abbreviated version.

The user's lexicon consists of a number of stored look-up words with subsequent pronunciation directions. The pronunciations could either be given as phonetic text codes or as normally spelled text.

The user's lexicon is chained to the language-specific file DFRULES. IVX (or XXRULES.IVX). XX stand for the language version (e.g. XX=AM for American English). The two chained files are downloaded on to the SA 201/PC card at the start-up of the system.

The lexicon file XXULEX.IVX is created with a special registration program, the editor ULEXED, which is provided on the SA 201/PC system diskette.

6.5   THE LEXICON EDITOR ULEXED

Since the lexicon file XXULEX.IVX is of a special format, it is necessary to use the special editor ULEXED to generate it. ULEXED is started with the command

ULEXED XX<cr>

where XX indicates the language used. Observe that the right language denomination has to be used in order to be able to chain the XXULEX.IVX file to the file XXRULES.IVX. XX must be the same for the two files. Thus, if we write the command:

ULEXED AM<cr>

the lexicon file with the name AMULEX.IVX is generated and then chained to AMRULES.IVX.

ULEXED XX sorts the look-up word into a list of look-up words with pronunciation directions for each. ULEXED uses the following six commands:

ABORT   <A>
EDIT   <E>
DELETE   <D>
LIST   <L>
PROMPT   <P>
QUIT   <Q>

ABORT: <A>
   With ABORT the program is terminated without any changes being stored.

EDIT: <E>
   The EDIT command can be used to change the lexicon file. EDIT prompts for look-up words and pronunciation directions.

DELETE: <D>
   The DELETE command deletes a look-up word with its pronunciation directions. Each deletion must be confirmed.

LIST: <L>
   The LIST command displays the content of the lexicon. CTRL-S is used to start/stop the listing.

PROMPT: <P>
The PROMPT command can be used to enter a message that will be displayed when the INITALK program is executed.

QUIT: <Q>
The QUIT command is used to terminate the program ULEXED. The file XXULEX is updated and the system returns control to the operating system of the computer.

6.5.1   Editor codes
ULEXED is a simple line editor. The program always operates in 'insert' mode. This means that the character written on the keyboard is inserted in the text at the position in front of the character marked with the cursor. The following codes can be used:

Arrow <--, -->
Backspace
CTRL-A
CTRL-D
CTRL-L
DEL
CTRL-G

Arrow:
Use the arrows to move the cursor in the text string. For example, if we have written the word Jon, we can press left arrow once and type an 'h' so that Jon becomes John.

Backspace:
Backspace deletes the character to the left of the cursor.

CTRL-A:
Same function as left arrow. This function is used on non-compatible computers.

CTRL-D:
Same function as right arrow. This function is used on non-compatible computers.

CTRL-L:
This code is used to listen to the pronunciation of a word in the lexicon.

DEL:
This code deletes the character indicated by the cursor.

CTRL-G:
This code performs the same function as the DEL key. It can be used on non-compatible computers.

7

A voice recognition language

7.1 INTRODUCTION

Ordinary programming languages such as FORTRAN, Pascal and COBOL process mainly numeric or character variables that are well defined in terms of the domains and ranges of values they can receive. However, with a voice-processing language the situation is completely different. Here, we process unpredictable incoming digital signals that correspond to the utterances we have produced, aiming to match these with the stored utterances.

In order to illustrate the processing of voice signals, we introduce a rather sophisticated voice-processing language (V.P.L.) which is offered by VOTAN, together with a voice card (the V.P.C. 2000).

The V.P.L. compiler, GEN, is a preprocessor which converts V.P.L. source file commands to executable code. To run GEN we type: GEN filename, where 'filename' is the name of the source file. The runtime executive, RUN, executes a V.P.L. program (i.e. the logic of the dialogue implemented). To execute a compiled V.P.L. program, we type: RUN filename, where 'filename' is the name of the executable code. To build a vocabulary, we use the so-called BLD system. BLD provides the means to: (a) create recognition templates and pre-record 'canned' messages, and (b) exercise and evaluate vocabularies and record messages in a controlled environment, outside the transaction itself (e.g. a fixed logic of a V.P.L. program). BLD is a menu-driven support package which allows the spoken words that are part of the application to be created and/or recorded, saved and evaluated.

The voice card can recognise (understand) the speech of any person speaking to it in any language, but first the voice card must be taught, or trained, to recognise the particular words or short phrases that are required.

Training consists of speaking a word or short phrase into the microphone. For example, the voice card can be trained to recognise the words 'save file', 'run DBase', 'setup', 'move cell', or any other words or phrases required to run the corresponding software. The voice card then makes a model, or 'template', of the spoken words. Later, when speech is used to run the software, the voice card compares the words spoken with the templates that have been created. If it finds a match, it 'recognises' the word, and the voice card and the host computer do whatever they have been set up to do when that word is recognised.

For example, let's say the voice card has been trained to recognise the word 'print' and link the spoken word 'print' with the key-strokes necessary for printing a file. When the word 'print' is spoken, the voice card will match that word with the template of the word 'print' in its memory, and then the name of a file can be typed.

The voice card recognises continuous speech, so the speaker does not need to use artificially long pauses between words in order for the voice card to tell when one word ends and another begins. This means that the speaker determines the rate of speech since the microphone is always 'listening'. Thus, the speaker is free of the artificial rhythm required by systems that can only recognise discrete words.

Another important feature of the voice card is its ability to interface with ordinary telephone lines and therefore provide the means to answer the telephone, record messages, and generally manipulate telephone signals using V.P.L. commands. V.P.L. provides eight commands to program telephone applications: ANSWER, DIAL, FLASH, OFFHOOK, ONHOOK, TONEIN, TONEOUT and TURN. However, before these commands can be used, a separate telephone card which is interfaced to the voice recognition card is necessary.

Since telephone company hardware systems vary greatly, there are some technical aspects of the telephone interface that need to be considered. The frequencies that can be monitored by V.P.L. commands are presented below.

When the DIAL command is used to initiate a call, the system looks for a dial tone, engaged signal, or a ringing tone when the number is being dialled. The dial tone should be composed of 350-Hz and 440-Hz tones. The engaged signal should be composed of 480-Hz and 620-Hz tones. The ringing signal should be composed of 440-Hz and 480-Hz tones. All these are dual-tone signals that overlap.

Telephone companies are required to maintain the above signals within plus or minus 1.5% of the levels described here. The voice card telephone interface can tolerate a variation of plus or minus 3% of the expected frequency. Manipulating the gain (see the GAININ parameter discussed later) will solve any problems regarding the ranges of the frequencies.

7.2   CONTINUOUS AND ISOLATED RECOGNITION

Isolated speech requires the user to speak each word with a distinct pause both before and after any word spoken for recognition. Continuous speech enables the user to speak a stream of words. This ability to speak naturally, without needing to introduce artificial sounding pauses into speech, can be a great advantage for certain applications.

With V.P.L. the system can be trained in two different modes: continuous and isolated. Note that words input under continuous mode can be recognised only under continuous mode and, similarly, words input under isolated mode can be recognised only under isolated mode.

The train/recognise continuous mode is selected by adding the CONTI-

NUOUS parameter to the TRAIN and RECOGNIZE commands. To select the isolated mode, the ISOLATED parameter is added to the TRAIN and RECOGNIZE commands, or the ISOLATED/CONTINUOUS parameter can be omitted; ISOLATED is the default.

Both isolated and continuous templates can be created for any template element, but each type is used only in its own context. Both of the V.P.L. modules BLD and RUN distinguish the two types internally.

When speaking in a continuous stream, the words are often distorted by the words around them. For example, in the sentence 'I'm going to Hertford', the word 'to' is more likely to sound like 'tuh'; a considerably different pronunciation from the clear 'to' when speaking the word by itself.

In order to get good results in continuous recognition, it is often necessary to create a word both alone (training of single words) and embedded in the middle of a stream of other words (training-in-phrases). The desired template is then extracted from the middle of the word stream and used as one of the reference templates. Training for template extraction can be done only through the V.P.L. BLD (Vocabulary Builder) program.

The voice card can accommodate an input that occupies about 22.5 kilobytes of memory, incuding templates that are created through the process of training-in-phrases. When training-in-phrases is adopted, and the maximum number of labels for phrases (64) is used, there will not be enough room to train the system twice for each word. However, it is rarely necessary to train-in-phrases any words except the digits and other very short words.

7.3   IMPROVING RECOGNITION ACCURACY

Recognition accuracy, that is, how many of the spoken words are recognised correctly by the system, depends on the speaker (i.e. his experience, and the choice of vocabulary words). The recognition accuracy should, generally, be over 98%, that is, for every 100 words in the vocabulary created, 98 or more of them should be recognised accurately. The following suggestions are made in order to obtain the best recognition accuracy possible.

(a)   Wait for the prompt (a beep sound), implying that the voice card is ready to accept input. Plan what is to be said ahead of time, wait for the beep, then speak the word without hesitating.

(b)   Create the templates under roughly the same conditions expected when using the system. For example, if a headset is to be used, then the voice card must be trained with a headset instead of with a hand-held microphone. Also, input the words under the same general noise level that is expected when using the system.

(c)   When the voice card is trained there is no need to speak in any special way. In fact, speech should be as normal as possible, with no special intonation or enunciation.

(d)   Speak clearly and in a firm tone, but do not exaggerate the words or shout.

(e)   Pay attention to the volume meter (a software window indicating the degree of volume) and keep the level within the box marked 'OK'.

(f)   The voice card recognises continuous speech best when the voice is crisp; a space between words, however small, is enough for the voice card to identify the end of one word and the beginning of another. For optimum accuracy, avoid a steady and monotonous tone that never 'turns off'.

(g)   Speed of delivery is not as important as crispness, but if the voice card cannot recognise speech satisfactorily, then slow down.

(h)   Speak directly into the microphone, not into its side. Follow the instructions that come with the microphone or headset regarding the distance this should be from the mouth.

(i)   If the microphone used has an on/off switch, turn it off when not in use. This will prevent the voice card from acting on commands that were not meant as input.

(j)   Choose words that are different from each other, in sound, for each set of templates that will be used together. Sometimes, words which do not sound similar to people sound similar to the voice card, so test thoroughly.

(k)   If there is a choice, longer words are better than shorter ones (longer words contain more distinctive information for the template).

(l)   Input each word twice, that is, speak it once, then go back over the words and speak each of them again. This is known as double training, a process that provides two templates for each spoken word. Double training is not strictly necessary, but it will help to increase the recognition accuracy.

(m)   The recognition accuracy of short words (like the digits) or words that sound very similar can be increased by using the training-in-phrases function. The idea is to speak a number of previously input words in a continuous stream (a 'phrase'). The voice card then extracts templates from the phrases and stores them with the other templates.

(n)   The templates generated have a long 'shelf life', that is, they will be capable of making a match with the input for a long time, six months or more. Although the templates should still be good if the speaker gets a cold or if he is very tired, it has been found that over a long period of time (at the very least, several months), the voice of the speaker changes sufficiently to necessitate re-training for best recognition accuracy.

7.4   DEFINITIONS AND GROUND RULES

V.P.L. is a high-level programming language designed for modestly skilled computer programmers and can be used to develop voice-based applications to run on the computer. (In Appendix B we present a complete application program written entirely in V.P.L. for a three-mail-box centre.)

The command set of V.P.L. includes: (a) declarations (i.e. statements preceeded by the symbol '#'), (b) commands and their optional parameters, and (c) sequence control statements. V.P.L. declarations declare dialogue elements and the text strings associated with dialogue elements; declarations must appear first in a V.P.L. program. The commands and sequence control statements that follow the declarations describe how the dialogue elements are to be manipulated to create a dialogue. In the next sections, V.P.L. commands and statements are explained using the following notations and conventions:

(a) Entities appearing within angle brackets <...> can be replaced by an equal value or entity.
(b) Within a rule, an optional element is indicated by enclosing it in brackets [...].
(c) Alternative elements are listed vertically within braces {...}.
(d) Each line of code may contain up to 128 characters; continuation lines are not allowed.

Upper and lower case letters
Lower or upper case can be used for the commands, buffers, parameters, and other words which are part of the V.P.L. syntax. However, element names must be used exactly as they appear when first defined, because case is significant.

Comments
Comments may be entered by using the exclamation symbol (!) as the first visible character on a line. It is advisable not to mix comments and commands on the same line.

Reserved words
Certain words are reserved for use with V.P.L. commands and it is therefore necessary to avoid using these in application programs. A full list of reserved words appears in Appendix C.

7.4.1 Distance (D1 and D2)

Distance is a score awarded to each incoming word and is a measure of how well a word spoken for recognition matches the stored templates. Distance is represented by values stored on the reserved variables D1 and D2, which stand for best distance and second-best distance. (these values will be seen when the Vocabulary Builder (BLD) is used).

The distance value is the difference, measured from 0 to 255, between the spoken word and the matching template. A good 'distance' for a match is between 0 and about 70 (the smaller the number is the better the match will be). The second-best distance is the distance between the spoken word and the second-best matching template. If D1 and D2 are close in value, (as they would be for the words 'stop' and 'top' for instance), the words are likely to get mixed up.

7.4.2   Acceptance

The acceptance limit is a threshold against which the incoming word is measured. The voice card considers any incoming word whose score is equal to or better (smaller) than the acceptance limit to be an acceptable match, and the word is recognised. If the score awarded for a template is larger than the acceptance limit, the template is not recognised.

The level at which acceptance is set can be altered by changing the acceptance level from the default of 70. If the voice card is judging the words too strictly, the acceptance level can be changed from the default of 70 to some higher number. Conversely, if the voice card is not judging the words strictly enough, the acceptance level can be changed from 70 to a lower number. The SETPAR command can be used to set the acceptance value globally, or the ACCEPT= parameter on the RECOGNIZE command to set the value for a particular section in the application program.

In some cases, a user may attempt to speak words that are not part of the templates available for matching. This situation may lead to false recognition of words within the template set. If it is very important to avoid false recognition and if it is difficult to control the end user, the solution is to lower the acceptance value.

7.4.3   Best word and second best word (W1 and W2)

Along with the best distance and second-best distance values we will see values for best word (expressed as W1) and second-best word (expressed as W2). These values are used in the BLD (Vocabulary Builder) routine. Best word, W1, is the number of the word that best matches the word spoken. The second-best word, W2, is the number of the word of the second-best match.

The best word and best distance values indicate how good a match has been achieved between the spoken word and the stored template. When mis-recognitions occur, these values will help to sort out the problem. It could be that there are two templates that are very similar; the solution is to choose a synonym for one of the words. Or maybe the word is spoken in a very different way than when it was input originally.

7.4.4   Gain

The gain is equivalent to the volume that indicates whether speech is too loud, too soft or just right.

V.P.L. allows the setting of the input and the output gain separately, using the GAININ and GAINOUT commands, or the GAIN= parameter on the SETPAR command with both input and output gain set to the same value; gain values range from 0 to 7.

Input gain affects the RECORD, SEND, TRAIN, and RECOGNIZE commands. Output gain affects the SAY (playback) and RECEIVE commands.

The SETPAR command is used to set the gain value globally. The

GAININ= parameter on the RECORD and/or SEND command, or the GAINOUT= parameter on the SAY and RECEIVE commands, are used to set the value at a particular section in the application program.

7.4.5 Bit rate

The bit rate is the number of bits per second of speech that the voice card generates to record messages. The rate is measured in thousands of bits per second, using the numbers 1 to 30; the default is 8 (i.e. 8000 bits per second).

Bit rate affects the RECORD and/or SEND command. Use the BITRATE= parameter on the SETPAR command to set the bit rate value globally, or use the BITRATE= parameter on the RECORD or SEND command to set the value for a particular section in the application program.

7.4.6 Naming V.P.L. files

The rules for naming V.P.L. source files and voice data files are the same as DOS 2.0 and 2.1 file-naming rules: the name of the dialogue can contain up to eight letters or numbers in addition to a disk designator. The system does differentiate between upper and lower case letters. File name extensions must not be included, because in certain cases described in the paragraphs that follow V.P.L. will add a file name extension. The general format of a DOS file name is:

drive:path\filename.ext

where 'drive' can be the letter 'A', 'B', etc., identifying a disk drive within the computer system, although most microcomputer systems have only two; 'path' defines the route through the directories above the one that contains the file proper; 'filename' can be up to eight letters or numbers; 'ext' is the extension of the filename and can be up to three letters or numbers. For example, the following are valid file names:

A:DIR1\MAILBOX.DAT

B:MAIL\JOHN\VPL1

Certain words are reserved and should not be used as dialogue or element names. These reserved words are listed in Appendix C.

When the V.P.L. source file is created using the text editor, the name of the V.P.L. file must match the dialogue name in the #def dialogue declaration (except for drive designator and path). For example, if the #def statement reads #DEF DIALOG Myfile, the name supplied to the text editor might read B:MYFILE (B: signifies the second floppy disk drive on a microcomputer).

When the V.P.L. source file is compiled by GEN, two files are created that are given the same name as the V.P.L. source file, with the V.P.L.-supplied extensions .PRC and .DIA.

When a voice data file is saved, any legal name can be assigned. V.P.L. supplies an extension of .DDT to template files, and .DDM to message files.

A vocoded voice data file is named for the element name specified. V.P.L. supplies an extension of .VOC, but the user can assign his own filename and extension.

7.4.7   Naming Elements
Elements within a dialogue must be named according to the following rules
(a)   The first character in the name must be alphabetic, after that, any character is valid except a comma or space.
(b)   An element name can contain up to eight characters.
(c)   Upper and lower case letters are distinguishable.

Certain words are reserved and should not be used as dialogue or element names. These reserved words are listed in Appendix C. The following are examples of valid element names:

        message3
        box#
        q328

7.4.8   Sets
The voice card can be directed to confine its search for the next recognition match to a particular group of templates. This group of templates is called a set. For example, if the user hears the message 'Enter your identification number', the application program might then issue a RECOGNIZE command that contains the name of a set called 'digits'. The set 'digits' would contain all of the templates that the user would accept as a legitimate recognition, presumably the digits zero to nine.

Sets are established using the '#def set' declaration. The user is encouraged to use sets, since using sets increases recognition accuracy; the system ignores all templates except those in the specified set. Response time is somewhat faster, since a smaller number of templates are examined. Programming will also be simplified, because the system culls out inappropriate responses.

7.4.9   Text strings
Text strings are used in text (#text) declarations and in MOVE, IF, ELSEIF, and DO WHILE sequence control statements.

Text strings must conform to the following rules:

(a)   Strings of printable characters must be placed within quotation marks.

(b)   Non-printable characters, such as representations of line feeds or carriage returns, must be individually represented by their decimal value within angle brackets, $<...>$. For example: $<13>$ represents a carriage return character; $<10>$ represents a line feed character.

(c)   Embedded quotation marks must be represented by double quotes (e.g. 'It was Socrates that said, "Know thyself." ').

(d)   Spaces are not permitted within a text string unless they are within quotes.

7.4.10   Buffers

Several built-in buffers are used in V.P.L.: RESP, COMM, TBUF, PARS, and B1–B8. These buffers may contain strings of ASCII characters. Although they can be referred to in a program, the names of the buffers are fixed. All buffers may contain up to 128 characters.

All the buffers can be manipulated identically. Any or all of the buffers can be used with the MOVE, APPEND, CLEAR and SHOW commands. RESP, COMM and TBUF can be used as general-purpose buffers, just like B1–B8, as long as we keep in mind the special purposes described below. The PARS buffer is a special case, as we explain later.

Numeric parameters can be passed in buffers; for example:

SETPAR GAININ= B1

The buffer must contain a string of ASCII numeric characters. An empty buffer, or a buffer containing only non-numeric characters, is interpreted as zero. If a value greater than the maximum for a particular parameter is entered, then the value is set to the maximum possible for that parameter. For example, in GAININ= B1, if B1 contains '123', input gain will be set to 7. No check is made for minimum value. The parameters affected are GAININ, GAINOUT, GAIN, BITRATE, ACCEPT, COUNT, ITIME, FTIME, TTIME, DELAY and RINGS. PROMPT can still use a buffer, but of course its contents are not numeric.

A buffer can also be used in a special way called 'indirect reference'. A description of indirect reference appears later.

7.4.10.1   Pseudo-buffers

In addition to string buffers, there are a number of 'pseudo-buffers' that can serve only as data sources; data cannot be written to these. So, pseudo-buffers, like PARS, can only appear on the left side of MOVE or APPEND (i.e., in the source position), as in MOVE PARS TO B8. The function of the various pseudo-buffers is to retrieve certain values in a readable/testable format. Pseudo-buffers move ASCII strings to string buffers.

The pseudo-buffers are the following:

PARS   — returns current gain settings, timeouts and other values.
FILELEN   — the length, in bytes, of the last disk file accessed by SAVE,
                SEND, RESTORE or RECEIVE.
RECTIME   — the approximate time, in seconds, of the most recent
                product of RECORD or SEND.
VERSION   — returns a string which indicates the voice card's firmware
                version numbers. The format of the string is 'CP Vnn.nn
                DSP Vnn.nn'.
MEMORY   — returns a string indicating the number of bytes of system
                memory available at any moment. This will help us make
                estimates of the space available for resident messages and
                templates.
KEYINT   — returns the character associated with the key stroke that
                most recently interrupted a voice or telephone function.

7.4.10.2   Response buffer

RESP is the response buffer. When a template is recognised, its response string, if any is assigned, is placed here. RESP is cleared on every recognition.

RESP is automatically cleared at the beginning of a TONEIN command, and the response string, if any, is appended to RESP for each tone detected during TONEIN.

7.4.10.3   Communications buffer

COMM is the communications buffer. When a template is recognised, its communications string, if any was assigned, is appended to this buffer. The TOHOST command transmits this buffer to the host, then clears it. The FROMHOST command replaces the contents of the COMM buffer with an ASCII string from the host.

COMM is not cleared automatically on every recognition. Rather, it is cleared when a TOHOST or CLEAR COMM is executed.

7.4.10.4   Tones buffer

TBUF is used for receiving push-button (DTMF) tones via the TONEIN command. When a tone is recognised, its tone string, if any, or its default tone string, is appended to the TBUF. TBUF is not cleared at the beginning of TONEIN.

7.4.10.5   General-purpose buffers

B1–B8 are general-purpose buffers which can be used as temporary storage locations for strings, or for other information.

7.4.10.6   Parameters buffer

PARS is an entity that functions much like a buffer. It can be moved (using the MOVE command) into a buffer, appended (using the APPEND command) to a buffer, or displayed with the SHOW command. When it appears in MOVE or APPEND, a string is moved which looks similar to this:

　　T00020　F00010　Z00600　G003　O003　A030
　　B008　W001　D020　W013　D084

Each letter in this string represents an operating parameter, followed by digits that vary according to the current value of the parameter. The letters and their meanings are described below:

T is the current timeout value set by the ITIME parameter
　　of certain commands.
F is the current value set by the FTIME parameter
　　of certain commands.
Z is the current value set by the TTIME parameter
　　of certain commands.
G is the current gain value set by the GAININ parameter
　　of certain commands.
O is the current gain value set by the GAINOUT parameter
　　of certain commands.
A is the current acceptance level set by the ACCEPT= parameter
　　of RECOGNIZE or SETPAR.
B is the current bit rate value set by the BITRATE= parameter
　　of various commands.
W is the word number of the most recently recognised template.
　　The first W represents the best match (W1) and the second W represents
　　the next best candidate (W2).
D is the distance value of the most recently recognised template.
　　The first D represents the distance value of the best match (D1) and the
　　next D represents the distance value of the next best match (D2).

The PARS string is useful because it can be moved or appended to the COMM buffer and transmitted to the host, or it can be moved to any buffer and examined by other V.P.L. commands. String values can also be manipulated from the PARS string. For example, the command:

　　　　MOVE PARS (48,3) to B1

moves the 48th, 49th, and 50th characters (the value for D1) to B1.
　　The command SHOW PARS displays the parameter values on the terminal or printout, but in a more easily readable form. For example, the PARS string we presented earlier would appear as:

```
Input gain . . . . . . . . . . . . . . . . . . .3
Output gain . . . . . . . . . . . . . . . . . .3
Bit rate . . . . . . . . . . . . . . . . . . . . .8000 bits/second
Acceptance level . . . . . . . . . . . . . . . .30
Time (initial) . . . . . . . . . . . . . . . . .20 seconds/10
FTIME (final). . . . . . . . . . . . . . . . .10 seconds/10
Latest best word . . . . . . . . . . . . . . .001
Latest best distance . . . . . . . . . . . . .020
Latest next best word . . . . . . . . . . . .013
Latest next best distance . . . . . . . . . .084
```

7.4.10.7   Indirect reference

Indirect reference permits a buffer name to be used in place of a filename, element, prompt, or set. The buffer then contains a character string which is the actual value to be used in the statement. For example, SAY GREET-ING is equivalent to:

        MOVE "GREETING" TO B1
        SAY B1

One common use of indirect reference is to allow a host or some group of V.P.L. statements to generate the name of a dialogue element in real-time, rather than 'hardcoding' that name during GEN. The following examples demonstrate some of the power of the indirect reference feature:

Example 1—Allow a host to decide what message to say next:

        FROMHOST   host supplies a name in COMM buffer;
        SAY COMM   any message can be said

Example 2—Produce a variable response based on a recognition event:

        RECOGNIZE SET7   assume this puts a string '4' in RESP
        MOVE "MSG" TO B1   B1 now contains MSG
        APPEND RESP TO B1
        SAY B1   message MSG4 is now played back in
                             response to the recognition

Example 3—Doing two recognitions, with the second dependent on the first:

        CLEAR COMM
        RECOGNIZE TOPSET
        MOVE "NEXT" TO B1
        APPEND RESP TO B1   B1 now contains NEXT based on first
                             recognition
        RECOGNIZE B1

| TOHOST | COMM will contain first response and the second dependent response |

Example 4—Training templates with prompts to guide user:

100: FROMHOST	assume host sends two-digit template "code"
IF COMM (1,1) EQ "*"	test for special condition to indicate end of training
GOTO 200:	
ENDIF	
MOVE "TEMP" TO B1	
APPEND COMM TO B1	B1 now contains TEMPxx
MOVE "CUE" TO B2	
APPEND COMM TO B2	B2 now contains CUExx
TRAIN B1 PROMPT= B2	
GOTO 100:	
200: FROMHOST	get name of that file
SAVE COMM	save under unique filename

7.4.11   Memory pointers

Memory pointers are symbolic representations of memory addresses that can be used with the LOAD, PART, RECEIVE or RESTORE commands. The letter "M" followed by a numeric value between 1 and 128 (as in "M12") indicates an address of our choice where the file resides. This address is symbolic only; when a memory pointer is used, V.P.L. performs all the management tasks necessary to allocate the memory required by the command.

7.4.12   Co-resident routines

A co-resident routine (co-routine) is an independent user-written program executing in the computer at the same time as a V.P.L. program. It can be written in Pascal, C or other high level programming language.

A co-routine and a V.P.L. program can communicate with each other through the COMM buffer, permitting the co-routine to provide functions that cannot be performed within V.P.L. programs. This is a very useful facility to have, since there will always be something that the user requires that cannot be directly implemented with the commands available in the standard system library. However, the non-expert user may not find the need to use co-routines.

7.5   DECLARATIONS

Declarations are not true commands but rather serve as instructions to GEN, appearing first in V.P.L. files. V.P.L. declarations are summarised in the following sections.

#def – dialogue declaration

The #def declaration names a dialogue and defines its elements. The following is a list of different declarations where the entry <word#> is an integer from 1 to 255:

#def	DIALOG	<dialogue name>
#def	TEMPLATE	<element name> [WORD=<word#>]
#def	MESSAGE	<element name> [WORD=<word#>]
#def	VOCODE	<element name> [WORD=<word#>]
#def	SET	<element name> [WORD=<word#>] <member, member...>

The first non-comment line in the V.P.L. source file must define the dialogue name with a #def statement. For instance, the first non-comment line in a V.P.L. source file named 'speech' would read:

#def dialogue speech

The dialogue name must be the same as the name assigned to the file when the text file was opened.

#text - text declaration

The #text declaration associates text strings with certain elements. The PROMPT string serves as a visual prompt when templates or record messages are created using BLD.

COMM and RESPONSE strings are associated with RECOGNIZE, and the #text declaration assigns these to elements. For example:

#text	<element name>	PROMPT="say alphabet"
#text	<element name>	COMM=<26>"abc"<26>
#text	<element name>	RESPONSE="alphabet"

#host – host declaration

The #host declaration defines the nature of a host system as follows:

#host SRL	Host is connected via an RS-232-C serial line
#host TERM	The default; host is keyboard/display
#host NONE	There is no host
#host USER	'Host' is a co-resident routine

Most serious applications require communications with another 'host' system. The type of host is declared once with a #host definition statement and V.P.L. thereafter manages the details of communications. The commands TOHOST and FROMHOST are used to indicate when communication is to occur in the application (these commands are discussed later).

#tone – tone declaration

The #tone declaration associates a text string for the RESP buffer (response string) and the TBUF buffer (tone string) for interfacing with telephone lines. These strings are appended to the buffers during the TONEIN command, for example:

> #tone <tone> RESPONSE= "tone1"
> #tone <tone> TONEBUF= "xyz"

The allowed values of <tone> are:

0, 1, 2, 3, 4, 5, 6, 7, 8, 9, *, #, A, B, C, D

7.6   V.P.L. COMMANDS

Each V.P.L. command and its permitted arguments are described in this section. Remember that all parts of a command must appear on a single line (maximum 128 characters).

ANSWER

ANSWER [DELAY= <time>] [TIME= <timeout>] [RINGS= <n>]

The ANSWER command is used to receive and answer incoming telephone calls. ANSWER closes the line so that the system is ready for an incoming call.

The optional DELAY= parameter is expressed in 100-millisecond units (tenths of seconds) and specifies the length of time between hanging up and successful completion of the ANSWER sequence. For voice, such a delay is usually not necessary.

The optional TIME= parameter is used to determine how long the ANSWER command will remain in effect if no call comes in before the command is completed. <timeout> is supplied in units of tenths of seconds; the maximum value is approximately 65 000 or about 1.6 hours, but the value can be set to infinity by setting TTIME to zero.

The optional RINGS= parameter determines how many rings the caller hears before the call is answered. If RINGS= is not included, the default value is four rings.

TIMEDOUT and NOT.OK flags are set if no call is received and the ANSWER command times out; NOT.TIMEDOUT and OK flags are set if an incoming call has been completed and is now in progress.

Examples   ANSWER DELAY   = 40 (4 seconds)
            ANSWER TTIME   = 3600 (1 hour)
            ANSWER RINGS   = 7 TTIME= 3600

APPEND

APPEND <string> TO <buffer>

APPEND a string to the contents of a buffer, or append the contents of a buffer to another buffer.

Examples:
> APPEND B1 TO COMM
> APPEND RESP(14,2) TO B4
> APPEND "abcdef" TO RESP

BEEP

BEEP causes the voice card to sound a 500-millisecond tone.

CLEAR

CLEAR <buffer>

Clear the indicated buffer by filling it with hexadecimal zeros.

Examples:
> CLEAR COMM
> CLEAR B3

CLEARLAST

CLEARLAST {<RESP>, <COMM>}

Clear the string most recently moved or appended to the COMM or RESP buffer. The CLEARLAST command can be used only with the COMM or RESP buffer.

The CLEARLAST command permits the removal of response and communications strings entered into buffers when a substitution or other error occurs with a RECOGNIZE command.

Examples: CLEARLAST COMM
            CLEARLAST RESP

DELETE

DELETE {<template>, <message> TEMPLATES, MESSAGES, ALL}

Delete templates or messages as follows:

DELETE <template> deletes a specific template in memory, where <template> is an element name. All templates, continuous and isolated, for that name are deleted.

DELETE TEMPLATES deletes all templates in memory.

DELETE <message> deletes a specific message in memory; <message> is an element name.

DELETE MESSAGES deletes all messages in memory.

DELETE ALL deletes all messages and templates in memory.

The template or message specified by <template> or <message> must have been previously defined by a #def declaration.

The parameter following DELETE can also be a buffer, in which case the buffer is presumed to contain the name of a template or message or the word TEMPLATES, MESSAGES, or ALL.

DIAL

DIAL <string> [RINGS= <n>]

The DIAL command is used to dial the number contained in the string or buffer indicated in <string>. The DIAL sequence is complete when the voice card detects a busy signal or voice, or rings the specified number of times (the default is four rings).

If a TURN ROTARY ON command has preceded the DIAL command, pulse dialling is used; otherwise push-button dialling is used. Push-button, or dual tone multi-frequency (DTMF) refers to tones sent or received by a 'push-button' telephone.

In addition to the phone number contained in <string> certain special codes can be used in conjunction with push-button (DTMF) dialling as follows:

W   — Wait for a dial tone. This might be incorporated when using a service such as SPRINT, which requires that more than one number be dialled (one to access SPRINT, another to reach the final destination). Another use might be when we want to reach an outside line through a PABX. Many of these systems require that we first dial a number ('9' is commonly used), then the number of our destination. If the switchboard or central telephone service uses a non-standard dial tone, use a P*n* at the beginning of the telephone number string.

P*n*   — Pause for *n* multiples of 100 ms (tenths of seconds), where *n* is a single digit 1...9.

W and Pn cannot be used for ROTARY dialling; only the digits can be used in the number.

The dialling sequence ends if one of the following conditions occurs:

(a)   The value set by the RINGS parameter is reached.

(b)   The voice card detects sound (OK flag is set).

The optional RINGS= <n> parameter indicates the number of times the voice card rings the telephone that is receiving the call. If the receiving telephone is not answered within the specified number of rings, the TIME-DOUT flag is set. The default value for <n> is four rings. The TIMEDOUT flag is also set if no ring is detected for the initial ten seconds of the call.

DIAL can also set two other testable flags. BUSY is set if the receiving telephone is busy. TIMEDOUT is set if the voice card gets no response (ringback, busy, or dial tone) within 20 seconds. NODIAL is set if no dial tone is detected within ten seconds.

The testable flag OK is set if the dial is completed and any sound is detected within the time limits. NOT.OK is set if the call fails or if the string is invalid.

Examples: DIAL "8009258000"
             DIAL "2684000P512500W4159604000"
             DIAL B4(10,10)
             DIAL COMM RINGS= 7

EXIT
Return system control to disk-operating system (DOS).

FLASH
FLASH has the same effect as pressing the button on the receiver cradle and then releasing it. The flash is one second long.

FROMHOST
FROMHOST [SOURCE= {SRL, TERM, USER, NONE}] TIME= <timeout>

FROMHOST directs the system to wait for a character string from the host and place it in the communications buffer (COMM). The received string may contain up to 128 ASCII characters of significance to the application, and must be terminated with an ASCII CR character (decimal 13). The string may itself contain meaning or may serve as a set of flags to be examined by subsequent commands to influence the logic of the voice application.

SRL represents serial communications, TERM represents the terminal, USER is a co-resident routine (as in the #host declaration), and NONE means there is no host. If no source is specified, TERM is used.

The SOURCE= parameter is optional; if it is omitted, the source established by the #host declaration prevails.

If the time specified in <timeout> is exceeded before any characters are received from the host, the TIMEDOUT flag is set. Otherwise, it is cleared. <timeout> is expressed in tenths of seconds; the maximum value of <timeout> is about 6550 seconds and the default is 60.

If the TIME= option is not present, FROMHOST will not return until an ASCII CR (carriage return) character is received.

Examples: FROMHOST
             SHOW COMM
             .
             .
             .
             FROMHOST

                    IF COMM(2,1) EQ "X"
                    GOTO 100
                    ELSEIF COMM(2,1) EQ "Z"
                    GOTO 200
                    ENDIF

LOAD
LOAD <filename> TO <address>

Read a voice data file (.DDT and/or .DDM) or vocode data file (.VOC)
from its source and store it in memory, beginning at the indicated address.
The complete file name must be provided, including the extension. The file
name can reside in a buffer.

The address is indicated by a memory pointer consisting of the letter 'M'
followed by any whole numeric value between 1 and 128. This memory
pointer is a symbolic representation of a memory address. When a memory
pointer is used, V.P.L. performs all the management tasks necessary to
allocate the memory required by LOAD.

If FEEDBACK is turned on and the memory space is not sufficient to
accommodate the file, then an error message will be displayed on the
monitor.

Examples: LOAD line4.voc TO M34
             LOAD myvoice.ddt TO M1
             MOVE "myvoice.ddt" TO B1
             LOAD B1 TO M1

MOVE
MOVE <string> TO <buffer>
Move a string to a buffer, or the contents of a buffer to another buffer. The
contents of the destination buffer are replaced by <string>.

Note that the MOVE command functions as a copy command (i.e., when
data is moved, the data still resides in the place it was moved from).

Examples:
             MOVE COMM to B4
             MOVE "abc" <10><13> "def" to B2
             MOVE B3(4,5) to B1

OFFHOOK
OFFHOOK opens the telephone line, that is, it performs the equivalent to
removing the handset from the hook. Incoming calls will encounter a busy
signal.

ONHOOK
ONHOOK unconditionally closes the telephone line, that is, it performs the
equivalent to putting the handset back on the hook, and terminates the call.
ONHOOK does not activate the voice card to receive incoming calls — the
ANSWER command does that.

PART
PART {TEMPLATES, MESSAGES, ALL} FROM {<filename>,
<memory pointer>}

Transfer voice data previously saved by the SAVE command from disk for
other storage) to the voice card without clearing information already
resident in the voice card. Messages or templates with the same word
number are replaced; others are not disturbed. V.P.L. looks for a file with
the extension .DDT or .DDM.

Note that the PART command does not clear information already
resident in memory; RESTORE clears all information from memory.

If the MESSAGES parameter is selected, only messages are restored.
V.P.L. restores files with the extension .DDM.

If the TEMPLATES parameter is selected, only templates are restored.
V.P.L. restores files with the extension .DDT.

ALL restores templates and messages — ALL is the default if TEM-
PLATES or MESSAGES is not specified. If ALL is selected, two restores
are done, on .DDT and .DDM files.

A memory pointer may be specified instead of a filename. However,
since individual files are loaded with LOAD, we must specify MESSAGES
or TEMPLATES if we restore from a memory pointer.

PART restores both isolated and continuous templates from the same
template file.

Examples: PART myvoice
             PART M15
             PART B2
             PART ALL FROM myvoice

RECEIVE
RECEIVE <filename> [GAINOUT= <value>]
This causes the voice card to play back previously vocoded material stored in
the file specified by <filename>. If a filename is not specified, <filename>
is assumed to be the name of a vocode element with the extension .VOC. If
<filename> includes an extension, V.P.L. looks for the complete name.

The output gain can be reset from its current value with the GAI-
NOUT= <value> parameter.

If the file was loaded to memory with the LOAD command, the memory
pointer that was assigned must be substituted for <filename>.

If a TURN VINT ON command was given and the message is interrupted by voice or other sound, the VOICEINT flag is set.

Example:

RECEIVE mytalk GAINOUT=4
LOAD mytalk.voc TO M13

.

.

.

RECEIVE M13 GAINOUT=4

RECOGNIZE
RECOGNIZE [{CONTINUOUS, ISOLATED} <set>]
[PROMPT= <message>] [GAININ= <value>] [ITIME= <timeout>]
[TTIME= <timeout>] [ACCEPT= <value>] [TERM= <template>]
[COUNT= <n>] [EVENT= <label>]

Continuous/isolated recognition
If the CONTINUOUS parameter is not included, ISOLATED recognition
is used.

Successful continuous recognition
A successful recognition of an individual word in continuous recognition
mode is called an "event". A successful recognition in continuous mode is
any sound heard by the voice card which produces a distance value that falls
below the acceptance level. The NOMATCH flag is not relevant to continuous recognition.

Failed Isolation Recognition
If the user does not respond within the specified time period, the TIME-
DOUT flag is set. The time specified in <timeout> temporarily overrides
the prevailing timeout period.

An inappropriate response (a response not a member of the set or, if no
sets are defined, in other words, an unrecognised response), causes the
NOMATCH flag to be set. If a match is made, the NOMATCH flag is
cleared.

Sets
The RECOGNIZE command expects a response which is a member of the
specified set. <set> is a dialogue element that is defined with a #def set
declaration. If a set is not specified, then all available templates are searched
for a match. While sets are not strictly necessary, their use is strongly
recommended. Using sets results in faster and more accurate recognition.

Prompts
<message> is the name of a defined element which is a recorded message. If
a prompt is specified, the recorded message is played before the user speaks
a word he wants recognised.

Input gain
GAININ sets the input gain; the range is 0 to 7.

Initial time
For isolated recognition, ITIME sets the amount of silence permitted at the
beginning of a recognition (i.e. the amount of time the voice card waits for
voice input). If the time specified is exceeded, the TIMEDOUT flag is set.
The value is expressed in tenths of seconds; the default is 30 (3 seconds). If
the value specified for ITIME is exceeded, the TIMEDOUT flag is set.

   For continuous recognition, ITIME represents the maximum amount of
silence allowed between events.

   The maximum permitted ITIME is 1.6 hours; 1 (one-tenth of a second) is
the minimum. To disable the ITIME test, set <timeout> to 0.

Total time
TTIME sets the total time permitted for a recognition. The value is
expressed in tenths of seconds; the default is 600 (60 seconds). TTIME has
significance both for isolated and continuous recognition.

   If the value specified for TTIME is exceeded, the TIMEDOUT flag is
set.

   The maximum permitted TTIME is 1.6 hours; 1 (one-tenth of a second)
is the minimum. To disable the TTIME test, set <timeout> to 0.

Terminate by template
TERM= applies only to continuous recognition. It specifies a template
which, when recognised, terminates RECOGNIZE. There is no default if
TERM= is omitted.

Terminate by count
COUNT= applies only to continuous recognition. It specifies a maximum
number of events before recognition is terminated. Recognition goes on
indefinitely if COUNT= is omitted or if n=0. The maximum value for
COUNT is 255.

Processing event by event
The EVENT= parameter applies only to continuous recognition.
EVENT= indicates a sequence of V.P.L. statements that are executed each
time a recognition event occurs. The sequence may not contain any voice
card functions such as TRAIN, RECORD, PLAYBACK, DIAL, etc., but
may include any other V.P.L. statements. The sequence must end logically
with either a RETURN statement or a STOP command. RETURN causes
the sequences to be repeated for the next unprocessed event. STOP

terminates recognition. If STOP is executed, the statement following the RECOGNIZE statement is the next command executed.

If the EVENT option is omitted, RESP will contain an accumulation of response strings upon termination of RECOGNIZE. That is, RESP is cleared for each recognition, but not for each event. If the EVENT option is included, RESP is cleared at the conclusion of each pass through the EVENT= sequence. In both cases, COMM is not cleared by each recognition; it is only cleared by TOHOST or CLEAR COMM.

Summary of termination conditions for continuous recognition
RECOGNIZE CONTINUOUS produces events until a termination condition occurs. A termination condition is one of the following

(a)   Number of events specified by COUNT= have occurred.
(b)   The template specified by TERM= is recognised.
(c)   The STOP command is encountered in the EVENT= sequence.
(d)   Amount of time specified by TTIME is exceeded.

Acceptance level
The acceptance level can be changed from its current value with the ACCEPT= parameter. Changing the acceptance level on the RECOGNIZE command does not change the level globally; to change the acceptance level globally, use SETPAR.

Communications or response strings
If a communications string was assigned to the recognised template, that string is appended to the communications buffer (COMM). Similarly, if a response string was assigned, that string is placed in (not appended to) the response buffer (RESP). RESP is cleared on each isolated recognition (see 'Processing event by event', above).

Feedback
If FEEDBACK is turned on, the name of the recognised template and the word number and distance of the best and second-best recognition candidates are displayed on the monitor. A message also displays if no match is found or if the recognition times out.
Examples:

        RECOGNIZE CONTINUOUS digits ITIME=60 ACCEPT=20
                TERM=quit EVENT=200
        RECOGNIZE ISOLATED digits PROMPT=asknum ITIME=40
                ACCEPT=20 TTIME=2000 GAININ=4
RECOGNIZE ITIME=40
RECOGNIZE

RECORD

RECORD <element>[PROMPT= <message>] [ITIME= <timeout>]
[FTIME= <timeout>] [TTIME= <timeout>] [GAININ= <value>]
[BITRATE= <value>]

This command records the message indicated by <element>. <message>
is the name of a defined element which is itself a recorded message. If a
prompt has been specified, the prompt is played before the RECORD is
performed.

A maximum time of 1.6 hours can be set for ITIME, FTIME and
TTIME. The minimum possible level is 1, equal to one-tenth of a second.
To turn off any time test, set the value to 0.

ITIME sets the amount of silence permitted at the beginning of a
recorded message (i.e. the amount of time the voice card waits for voice
input). The voice card is not recording silence during this time; it is just
waiting for voice input. If the time specified is exceeded, the TIMEDOUT
flag is set. The value is expressed in tenths of seconds; the default is 30 (3
seconds).

FTIME sets the amount of silence permitted at the end of a recorded
message. If the time is exceeded, vocoding ceases. The value is expressed
in tenths of seconds; the default is 15 (1.5 seconds).

TTIME sets the total time permitted for recording. The value is
expressed in tenths of seconds; the default is 600 (60 seconds).

The input gain can be reset from its current value with the GAININ=
<value> parameter. The <value> must be within the range 0 to 7.

The BITRATE= <value> parameter can be used to reset the bit rate
at which recording takes place. The <value> must be within the range 1
to 30.

Examples: RECORD myname PROMPT=speakup GAIN=5
              RECORD myname

RESTORE

RESTORE { MESSAGES, TEMPLATES, ALL } [FROM]
{ <filename>, <memory pointer> }

The RESTORE command clears all templates and/or messages in memory
and then transfers data previously saved by the SAVE command.

Note that the PART command does not clear information already
resident in memory; RESTORE clears all information from memory.

If the file has been loaded to memory with the LOAD command, the
assigned memory pointer may be substituted for <filename>. However,
since individual files are loaded with LOAD, we must specify MESSAGES
or TEMPLATES if we restore from a memory pointer.

If the MESSAGES parameter is selected, only messages are restored
(these are files with the extension .DDM).

If the TEMPLATES parameter is selected, only templates are restored
(these are files with the extension .DDT).

ALL restores templates and messages.

RESTORE restores both isolated and continuous templates from the same template file.

Examples: RESTORE myvoice
             LOAD myvoice.ddt TO M13

             .
             .
             .

             RESTORE MESSAGES FROM M13

SAVE
SAVE { MESSAGES, TEMPLATES, ALL } [TO] <filename>

This transfers voice data from the voice card to the disk (or other storage).
If the MESSAGES parameter is selected, only messages are saved. V.P.L. assigns the extension .DDM.
If the TEMPLATES parameter is selected, only templates are saved. V.P.L. assigns the extension .DDT.
ALL saves templates and messages. ALL is the default if TEMPLATES or MESSAGES is not specified.
SAVE saves both isolated and continuous templates in the same template file.
If the destination disk is full, the FULL flag is set.

Example: SAVE MESSAGES myvoice

SAY
SAY <element> [GAINOUT= <value>]

Play back the message specified in <element. The output gain can be reset from its current value with the GAINOUT= parameter.
If a TURN VINT ON command was given and playback is interrupted by voice or other sound, the VOICEINT flag is set.
Example: SAY question GAIN=5
            SAY intro

SEND
SEND { <element>, <filename> } [GAININ= <value>]
[ITIME= <timeout>] [FTIME= <timeout>] [TTIME= <timeout>]
[BITRATE= <value>]
Record voice for vocoding and transfer the voice data to a disk file. If a filename is not specified, <filename> is assumed to be the name of a vocode element with the extension .VOC. If <filename> includes an extension, V.P.L. looks for the complete name.
The input gain can be reset from its current value with GAININ= <value>. The range is 0 to 7; the default is 3.

A maximum time of 1.6 hours may be set for ITIME, FTIME and TTIME. The minimum timeout is 1, equal to one-tenth of a second. To turn off any time test, set the value to 0.

ITIME sets the amount of silence permitted at the beginning of a vocoded message (i.e. the amount of time the voice card waits for voice input). If the time specified is exceeded, the TIMEDOUT flag is set. The value is expressed in tenths of seconds; the default is 30 (3 seconds).

FTIME sets the amount of silence permitted at the end of a vocoded message. If the time is exceeded, vocoding ceases. The value is expressed in tenths of seconds; the default is 15 (1.5 seconds).

TTIME sets the total time permitted for vocoding. The value is expressed in tenths of seconds; the default is 600 (60 seconds).

If a turn VINT ON command was given and playback is interrupted by voice or other sound, the VOICEINT flag is set.

The recording bit rate may be changed by BITRATE= <value>. The default is 8 (8000 bits per second). The range is 1 to 30.

If the destination disk is full, the FULL flag is set.

A SEND operation is terminated by striking any key, or if the time specified by TTIME or FTIME is exceeded. Under any of these conditions, the TIMEDOUT flag is not set and the message is preserved.

Examples: SEND mytalk GAIN=4 BITRATE=6
             SEND mytalk BITRATE=6
             SEND mytalk.abc

SETPAR
SETPAR [ITIME≡ <value>] [FTIME≡ <value>] [TTIME= <value>]
[{GAIN= <value>}, {GAININ= <value>, GAINOUT= <value>}]
[BITRATE= <value>] [ACCEPT= <value>] [KEYINT= <value>]

A maximum time of 1.6 hours may be set for ITIME, FTIME and TTIME. The minimum timeout is 1, equal to one-tenth of a second. To turn off any time test, set the value to 0.

ITIME sets the amount of silence permitted at the beginning of voice input. If the time specified is exceeded, the TIMEDOUT flag is set. The value is expressed in tenths of seconds; the default is 30 (3 seconds).

FTIME sets the amount of silence permitted at the end of voice input. If the time is exceeded, the TIMEDOUT flag is set. The value is expressed in tenths of seconds; the default is 15 (1.5 seconds).

TTIME sets the total permitted for voice input. The value is expressed in tenths of seconds; the default is 600 (60 seconds).

GAIN sets the value for both input gain and output gain. If the GAIN parameter is used, the GAININ and/or GAINOUT cannot be used.

GAININ sets the input gain for training, recording and vocoding.

GAINOUT sets the input gain for playback (SAY or RECEIVE).

BITRATE sets the value for the bit rate, in thousands of bits per second. The value must be between 1 and 30; the default is 8 (8000 bits per second).

ACCEPT sets the value for acceptance. The value must be between 0 and 255. The default is 70.

KEYINT indicates which key (character) may interrupt a function. Non-printable ASCII characters (such as Ctrl-C) may be represented by their decimal value (<3> for Ctrl-C). Case is ignored for alphabetic characters, so KEYINT=a and KEYINT=A mean the same thing. KEYINT=<0> means any key may interrupt.

SHOW
SHOW {<buffer>, <"a literal string of characters">}

Display on the monitor the contents of the specified buffer, or a literal string of characters.

The buffer PARS is a special case. A formatted display is shown of the current values for various parameters, such as acceptance level, input gain, output gain, timeout, etc.

The state of the FEEDBACK toggle does not affect SHOW.

Examples: SHOW COMM
             SHOW PARS
             SHOW "Please say the password"

STOP
STOP terminates RECOGNIZE from an EVENT= sequence. STOP is used only with the RECOGNIZE CONTINUOUS command.

TOHOST
TOHOST [DEST= { SRL, TERM, USER, NONE }]

Transfer the contents of the communications buffer (COMM) to the host, and clear the buffer. The transmitted string may contain up to 128 ASCII characters of significance to the application.

The DEST= parameter defines the location of the host and is optional. If it is omitted, the default established by host declaration prevails.

SRL represents serial communications, TERM means the monitor, USER means the co-resident user's job, and NONE means no destination.

Example: TOHOST

TONEIN
TONEIN [COUNT= <n>] [TIME= <timeout>] [TERM= <tone>]

TONEIN commands the voice card to detect and collect incoming 'push-button' (DTMF) tones. A telephone call must be in progress for TONEIN to function. When a tone is detected by the voice card the tone string (if any) or its default value is appended to the TBUF buffer. The response string (if any) is appended to the RESP buffer. The RESP buffer is cleared at the beginning of TONEIN, but the TUBF is not automatically cleared.

The user will not hear a 'beep' to propmpt him to enter tones. It is suggested that the TONEIN command be preceded with a BEEP command.

Reception of tones is terminated by one of the three optional parameters COUNT, TIME and TERM, as follows:

The COUNT= parameter determines the number of tones that can be detected before the TONEIN command is completed. There is no default limit on the number of tones; however, tones will no longer be appended to the TBUF and RESP if those buffers are filled and the special flag FULL is set. The default is one (1).

The TIME= parameter specifies (in tenths of seconds) the length of silence required to end the TONEIN command. The default is 60 (6 seconds). The maximum time is about 25 seconds.

The TIMEDOUT flag will be set if TONEIN is terminated due to the TIME parameter. OK is set if any tones were detected; NOT.OK will be set if no tones were detected.

The TERM= parameter causes the TONEIN command to terminate if the indicated <tone> is detected on the line. That final tone will be placed in the two buffers.

Examples: TONEIN COUNT=5
             TONEIN TERM=#
             TONEIN TERM=* COUNT=20 TIME=30

TONEOUT
TONEOUT <buffer>

TONEOUT sends 'push button' (DTMF) tones over the telephone line; a call must be in progress for the command to function. <buffer> can be any buffer or a string. The following values are allowed in the <buffer>:

$$0, 1, 2, 3, 4, 5, 6, 7, 8, 9, *, \#, A, B, C, D$$

It is recommended that the GAINOUT= parameter on the SETPAR command be set to 4 or 5 in order to ensure that TONEOUT will work.

Examples: TONEOUT "845##900*CD"
             TONEOUT COMM
             TONEOUT B1(4,5)

TRAIN
TRAIN [{ CONTINUOUS, ISOLATED }] > <element>
[PROMPT= <message>] [ITIME= <timeout>] [TTIME= <timeout>]
[GAININ= <value>]

This command is used to train the system to recognise the template indicated by the element name.

CONTINUOUS/ISOLATED is an optional parameter. If it is omitted, the default is isolated training. Templates trained in one mode (isolated or continuous) can be recognised only in the same mode.

<message> is the name of a defined element which is a recorded message. If a prompt is specified, that message is played before the TRAIN is performed.

A maximum time of 1.6 hours may be set for ITIME and TTIME. The minimum timeout is 1, equal to one-tenth of a second. To turn off any time test, set the value to 0.

ITIME sets the amount of silence permitted at the beginning of a message (i.e. the amount of time voice card waits for voice input). If the time specified is exceeded, the TIMEDOUT flag is set. The value is expressed in tenths of seconds; the default is 30 (3 seconds).

TTIME sets the total time permitted for training. If the time specified is exceeded, the TIMEDOUT flag is set. The value is expressed in tenths of seconds; the default is 600 (60 seconds).

GAININ sets the input gain. The allowed range is 0 to 7; the default is 3.

Examples: TRAIN digit
             TRAIN CONTINUOUS me PROMPT=mess1
             TRAIN start ITIME=40

TURN

TURN can be used to select a number of conditions: feedback, automatic gain control, beeps, and certain telephone conditions, as follows:

TURN FEEDBACK { ON, OFF }

TURN can be used as a 'switch' to turn feedback on or off. Various commands provide visual feedback on the monitor such as error messages or other messages. The default is ON.

TURN PHONE { ON, OFF }

Resets the audio path for input and output for the telephone instead of the microphone. The speaker is still active.

TURN ROTARY { ON, OFF }

TURN ROTARY ON indicates that rotary (pulse) dialling is used in the DIAL command; ROTARY OFF (the default if no TURN ROTARY command is present) indicates push-button (DTMF) dialling is to be used. ROTARY does not affect the TONEOUT command. The default is OFF.

TURN AGC { ON, OFF }

Automatic gain control (AGC) compensates for variation in input volume by adjusting the dynamic range of the system. The default is OFF for voice and telephone functions.

TURN VINT { ON, OFF }

TURN VINT ON permits the user to use speech or any sound to interrupt a message (SAY, RECEIVE) being played back. If a message is interrupted by speech, the VOICEINT flag is set.

TURN BEEP { ON, OFF }

TURN BEEP OFF turns off all beeps except those entered with the BEEP command. The beeps are ON when the system is booted. TURN BEEP ON restores all beeps and is the default.

TURN KEYINT { ON, OFF }

TURN KEYINT OFF disables the ability to interrupt voice and telephone functions with key-strokes. TURN KEYINT ON restores it.

TWAIT
TWAIT [TTIME= <timeout>]

This command waits for one of the following to occur:
(a)   TTIME to expire, in which case the TIMEDOUT flag is set.
(b)   A key-stroke. This will interrupt TWAIT only if TURN KEYINT ON is in effect.

If TURN PHONE ON (or AUDIO09–AUDIO15) and TURN KEYINT ON are in effect, then one of the following will occur:

(c)   The receiver is removed from the hook. SETONHOOK will be false.
(d)   The receiver is replaced. SETONHOOK is true.
(e)   An incoming call is detected. RINGING is true.
Note that SETONHOOK always reflects the current state of the receiver as long as TURN PHONE ON and TURN KEYINT ON are in effect. The SETONHOOK flag is false if the receiver is off-hook. For example, if TWAIT times out while the receiver is on-hook, SETONHOOK will be true even though placing the receiver on-hook is not what terminated TWAIT.

7.7   SEQUENCE CONTROL STATEMENTS

Sequence control statements and statement labels permit the structuring of dialogues. The commands are very similar to commands found in every high-level programming language and will be quite familiar to programmers.

Sequence control statements may be nested to 128 levels and allow the following:

(a)   Conditional execution of command lines (IF, ELSE, ELSEIF).
(b)   Subroutines (CALL, RETURN).
(c)   Structured iterations (DO n TIMES, DOWHILE).
(d)   Simple branching (GOTO).

Labels are used with the CALL and GOTO statements.

Two types of expressions, string comparisons and flags, are used by the sequence control statements.

An explanation of expressions and descriptions of each sequence control statement follows.

Expressions

IF, ELSEIF and DO WHILE statements evaluate an expression to determine whether to execute the command lines which follow. An expression does one of two things: (a) compares one string to another, or (b) evaluates the state of a flag.

String comparisons

The first string is indicated by a buffer name (COMM, RESP, Bn, etc). The buffer name may be followed by a pair of numbers enclosed in parentheses and separated by a comma. This number pair indicates that a sub-string of the string in the indicated buffer is to be compared. The first number is the index of the first character of the sub-string. The second number is the number of characters to be included in the sub-string comparison.

The second string may also be contained in a named string buffer, or it may be a sub-string, or it may be a literal string. Literal strings are enclosed in quotation marks.

The comparison symbol itself must be one of the following:

EQ   – equals
GE   – greater than or equal
GT   – greater than
LE   – less than or equal
LT   – less than
NE   – not equal

The strings are compared, character by character, and the relationship between them is evaluated. V.P.L. then determines which string is lower in the ASCII collating sequence. No mathematical calculations take place.

Examples: IF COMM EQ B1
            IF COMM(2,3) EQ "STR"
            ELSEIF B1(3,2) LT COMM

Flag status

The second kind of expression describes the status of a simple 'flag'. For example, IF TIMEDOUT means that the expression is true if the most recent RECOGNIZE command timed out.

The following flags are permitted as expressions:

TIMEDOUT is true if the most recent RECOGNIZE or TRAIN timed out.
TIMEDOUT is also true:

(a)   if the DIAL command is ringing the phone, but no answer is heard;
(b)   if the ANSWER command does not detect an incoming call;
(c)   if TONEIN is not completed within its time limit.

NOT.TIMEDOUT is true if the most recent RECOGNIZE or TRAIN did not time out. NOT.TIMEDOUT is also true:

(a)   if the DIAL command completed a call;
(b)   if ANSWER received a call;
(c)   if TONEIN is terminated by either COUNT or TERM, rather than the time limit.

NOMATCH is true if the most recent RECOGNIZE command did not find a match.

FULL is true if the computer's memory is full; the FULL flag is set by record or TRAIN. FULL is also true if the TONEIN fills the TBUF or RESP buffers. FULL is set by SAVE and SEND when the disk is full.

BUSY is true if the DIAL command detected a busy signal on the receiving line.

NODIAL is true if the DIAL command was unable to detect a dial tone.

OK is true: if tones were detected during TONEIN, the DIAL command is completed and a call is now in progress, and if an ANSWER command has answered an incoming call

NOT.OK is true if some error or unusual condition prevented a command from completing in the normal fashion.

KEYINT is true if the most recent voice or phone function was interrupted by a key-stroke.

SETONHOOK is true if TURN KEYINT ON was in effect and the most recent voice or telephone function was interrupted because the receiver was placed on hook. It is false if the receiver was taken off the hook.

RINGING is true if TURN KEYINT ON was in effect and the most recent voice or phone function was interrupted because an incoming call was detected.

VOICEINT is true if SAY or RECEIVE was interrupted by voice input while TURN VINT ON was in effect.

GOTO
GOTO <label>

In V.P.L., <label> is a user-defined number assigned to lines of V.P.L. code for use by a GOTO or CALL statement. The V.P.L. label must be greater than 0 and less than 1000, and followed by a colon (:).

The label indicates the next command line. This is a simple branch.

While GOTO commands can be very useful, they are also easily over-used to the point of obscuring the logic of the application. Therefore, they must be used sparingly.

Example: GOTO 500:

RETURN
RETURN takes as the next command line the line following the most recent CALL line encountered. RETURN is also used for continuous recognition.

CALL
CALL <label>

In V.P.L., <label> is a user-defined number assigned to lines of V.P.L. code for use by a GOTO or CALL statement. The V.P.L. label must be greater than 0 and less than 1000, and followed by a colon (:).
    The label on the CALL command specifies the next command line. The next RETURN command encountered causes the interpeter to take as the next command line the one following the last CALL line. Note that CALL statements may be nested to 128 levels.

Example: CALL 100:

             .

             .

             .

             100: RECOGNIZE yesno TIME=20
             RETURN

IF...ELSE
IF...ELSE...ENDIF

If the value of the expression following the IF is true, command lines are executed from the one which follows the IF to the one before the optional ELSE. Then the command lines following the ENDIF are executed.
    If the value of the expression following the IF is false, the command lines which follow ELSE are executed. If ELSE is not present and the test is false, the next command line is that which follows ENDIF. Note that IF commands may be nested to 128 levels.
    The following points should be taken into consideration when using IF statements:
(a)   A GOTO within the IF is legal when the GOTO indicates a label totally outside the IF.
(b)   A GOTO which indicates a label within the IF, while not strictly illegal, should be avoided.
(c)   A CALL within the IF is proper, unless it fails to RETURN.

IF...ELSEIF
IF...ELSEIF...ELSEIF...ELSE...ENDIF

IF introduces the first of a series of conditional expressions. Subsequent expressions are introduced by each ELSEIF. Only the commands between the first true IF or ELSEIF expression and the next ELSEIF or ENDIF command lines are executed. The last conditional in this series can be an

ELSE. Note that IF commands may be nested to 128 levels. The same points we presented for the IF...ELSE...ENDIF command must be taken into consideration when using the IF...ELSE... command.

DO n TIMES
DO n TIMES...ENDDO

Here, the command lines between the line containing the initial DO and the final ENDDO are executed n times. Note that, the DO n TIMES statements may be nested to 32 levels. The following points must be taken into consideration when using the DO command:

(a)   A GOTO within the DO which indicates a label outside the DO terminates the DO even if it has not been repeated the required number of times. Thus a GOTO can be used the same way a BREAK or CONTINUE statement might be used in a structured programming language.

(b)   A CALL does not terminate the DO unless it fails to RETURN (not a recommended practice).

DO WHILE
DO WHILE <expression>...ENDDO

The command lines between <expression> and the final ENDDO are executed repeatedly until <expression> is false. The <expression> can include buffer names compared to other buffer names, but two strings cannot be compared. Note that DO WHILE statements may be nested to 128 levels.

In V.P.L., a label is a user-defined number assigned to lines of V.P.L. code for use by a GOTO or CALL statement. The V.P.L. label must be greater than 0 and less than 1000, and followed by a colon (:).

The same points presented under the DO n TIMES command should be considered when using the DO WHILE command.

APPENDIX A: A program to convert words to phonemes

A.1 INTRODUCTION

The program CONVERT takes as its input a word, and produces as its output the corresponding phonetic transcription. This tranformation is achieved by applying a set of rules to each letter in the word; the rules determine the phoneme(s) generated by the letters.

The rules are based on those originally published by Elovitz *et al.* (1976), with some alterations. Each letter has its own list of rules, some letters requiring several rules, whilst others only one or two. A full listing of all the rules used here is presented at the end of this appendix, in the required format for the program CONVERT.

The best way to understand how the rules operate is to work through an example by hand, using the word:

BEWARE
↑

The first letter is 'B' and therefore the rules applying to this letter must be searched for a match. It is important to search the rules in the order they are listed: exceptions first and more general rules second. The first matching rule applying to letter 'B' is rule number 34, having the following form:

2　　$E!#　　34 /b ih/

The letter 'B' is not included in the rule but is assumed to be between the symbols '$' and 'E'. The rule could in fact have taken the form:

2　　$[B]E!#　　34 /b ih/

where the letter under consideration is enclosed in square brackets ([ ]). There is a maximum of five symbols preceding, and a maximum of six symbols following the letter 'B' in the above rule. The first five characters apply to any letters preceding the letter under consideration, and the next six apply to those following the letter. In the above rule, the symbol '$' is equivalent to a space, the symbol '!' is equivalent to one consonant, and the symbol '#' is equivalent to one or more vowels.

The rule could have been written in English as:

When the letter 'B' is preceded by a blank space, the letter immediately following the letter 'B' is the letter 'E'; the letter 'E' is followed firstly by one consonant and secondly by one or more vowels; then the letter 'B' is allocated the phoneme represented orthographically by /b/. Further, the letter 'E' in these circumstances is allocated the phoneme represented orthographically by /ih/.

The number 34 is used purely as an identifier of the rule within the rules file. The phonemes are enclosed between two slashes (/ /).

The number 2 indicates that the next letter requiring examination within the word under consideration is two letters from the current one. This takes us to letter 'W':

> BEWARE
>

The rules for the letter 'W' must now be checked in lexical order. The first matching rule is rule number 292, which has the following format:

> 3   AR   292/w ao r/

This states that:

When the letter 'E' is immediately followed by the letters 'AR' (in that order), then it is allocated the phoneme represented orthographically by /w/. Further, the letter 'A' in these circumstances is allocated the phoneme represented orthographically by /ao/, and the letter 'R' is allocated the phoneme orthographically represented by /r/.

The advance in this case is three forward, taking us to the letter 'E':

> BEWARE
> ↑

The rules for the letter 'E' are then checked in lexical order. The first matching rule is rule number 64, with the following form:

> 1   #:$ 64/ /

This states that:

When the letter 'E' is immediately preceded by zero or more consonants and these consonants are themselves immediately preceded by one or more vowels, and in addition, the letter 'E' is also followed by a space (indicating the end of a word), then the letter 'E' is silent. In other words, it is not allocated a phoneme.

The advance in these circumstances is one, taking us past the end of the word, thus indicating that the process is finished.

The phonemes that have been allocated are:

/b/ /ih/ /w/ /ao/ /r/

The rules are organised in such a way that the last rule applicable to each letter is a default rule which will always match. This rule is therefore used when all the other rules have failed. In the above example, a default rule was not encountered because a match was found each time.

Each set of rules starts with the letter which the subsequent rules apply to and is terminated by the number '9' (see Appendix A.4). This is so that the program 'CONVERT' can read in the rule file correctly.

An outline flow chart for the program 'CONVERT' is presented in Fig. A.1, representing the major steps of the logic of the program in the following manner:

(1) Read into memory the file containing all the rules and their associated phonemes.
(2) Accept a source word from the input file.
(3) Convert the letters of the source word into their corresponding phonemes.
(4) Output the phonemes (e.g. on to V.D.U. or voice synthesis device).
(5) Repeat step 2 above to the end of the sentence/paragraph/input.

The program itself is fully documented with all the variables explained within the source, including a brief outline of the purpose of each procedure/function.

In the following we discuss briefly the procedures/functions of the program CONVERT which implements the steps outlined in Fig. A.1, together with some of the design considerations.

A.2   PROGRAM LOGIC

A.2.1   Read in all the rules

This is accomplished in the procedures 'insertintorule' and 'readinnew'. The rules for each letter are read into linked lists, each letter being allocated its own linked list. The lists are accessed via an array 'A'..'Z' of type linked list. Each element of the list is a record which contains appropriate slots for:

(a)   the rule consisting of the various symbols;
(b)   the phonemes generated by each rule;
(c)   the advance to obtain the position of the next letter to be converted;

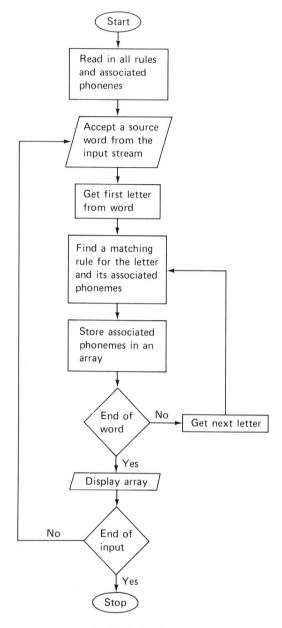

Fig. A.1 — Outline logic of program 'convert'.

(d)   a number to identify each rule; this could in fact be excluded, but it is
       very useful from the point of view of error checking.

Recursion is used to create the linked lists as the rules are read in. This
means that each list can be variable in length and therefore hold as many
rules as are applicable to each letter.

To enable the program to determine the correct list, each block of rules for a given letter starts with that letter on a line by itself, and is terminated by the number '9' appearing on a separate line.

A.2.2 Accept a source word from the input stream

The procedure 'readword' accepts a word from the input (e.g. file or keyboard). The word read is transferred into a packed array of 31 characters long (0...30), starting from position 1 onwards. Position 0 is used to hold the 'space' character which marks the beginning of a word.

As the letters of each word are read in they are processed further as follows: (1) they are checked to make sure that they are alphabetic; a non-alphabetic character, including hyphen, is assumed to mark the end of the word; (2) they are converted to upper case letters. The reason for the conversion is that it makes the rule-matching process easier later on.

The procedure 'makeupper' converts lower-case letters to upper-case, where the value 32 is the difference between the ordinal values for upper- and lower-case letters. If the user intends to run the program on a different character set, it is advisable to check this value on the character set of the computer in use.

A function called 'apostrophe' has also been included to distinguish apostrophes from single inverted commas. This is necessary, since free running text often contains inverted commas which have to be distinguished from apostrophes in order to apply the correct matching rule.

An error message is generated if a word longer than 23 characters is encountered; the longest word in the English dictionary we have used for research is 'anthropomorphologically', with 23 letters.

In conclusion, the input to the program can be in either upper or lower case; punctuation marks and other non-alphabetic characters will be ignored. The words can either be entered via the keyboard or from a text file, depending on what is assigned to the default INPUT when the program is run. One word can be entered, or a string of words (as found in free running text).

A.2.3 Get a letter from the word and find a matching rule

This is all part of the rule-matching process which is accomplished by the procedure 'searchformatch' and the function 'checkformatch'.

The procedure 'searchformatch' is used to check the rules (for a given letter) in lexical order. If the first rule does not match then the procedure calls itself recursively, by passing the location of the next rule in the list. If this rule does not match, the procedure is re-entered until a rule is found that does match. The last rule of each linked list containing the rules for a given letter has been designed in such a way as to ensure that it will always match; this is the default rule used when all the other rules have failed.

In order to check the symbols in the rules with the letters in the word being converted, the procedure 'searchformatch' calls the function 'check-formatch'. This is a Boolean function which will return the value 'true' only if a symbol has been successfully matched against the appropriate letter.

Certain problems arise in the matching process because one symbol may have to be checked against more than one letter. For example, the symbol '#' indicates that one or more vowels has to be checked for. The symbol ':', on the other hand, indicates that zero or more consonants are to be checked for. Other symbols require that specific letter combinations are to be checked, such as '%', which requires that a suffix is checked for. Another problem is that if the symbol occurs in the part of the rule that applies to the preceding letters, it has to be processed in the opposite way than if it had occurred in that part of the rule which applies to succeeding letters. Note that preceding letters are checked right to left, and succeeding letters are checked left to right. The problem of deciding which way to check the symbols against the letters is overcome by passing a $+1$ or -1 to the function when it is called. This value can then be utilised to determine the direction of the checking process.

In an effort to demonstrate the problems outlined above, we assume that the following part of a word is being checked:

$$-TEALE-$$
$$\uparrow$$

Let the current part of a rule under consideration be as follows:

$$!\#:[E]$$

where [E] indicates that it is a rule for the letter 'E', and the symbols are to be checked against the letters preceding the letter 'E'. The symbol ':' would need to be checked against the letter(s) immediately preceding [E], which in this case is 'L'. A match is found, since the letter 'L' is a consonant. The symbol '#' would then need to be checked against the letter 'A'. This again would match, since the letter 'A' is a vowel. However, the rule states that one or more vowels have to be checked for, and consequently the first 'E' has again to be checked against the symbol '#' for a match, which is found here. The next letter would also need to be checked against the symbol '#', which in this example is the letter 'T'. On this occasion the matching process would fail, since the letter 'T' is not a vowel.

Overall, the above matching process has succeeded, as the rule states that one or more letters have to match for the rule to succeed. The next step, therefore, is to check the letter 'T' against the symbol '!', which in fact determines the presence of one consonant. The letter 'T' is a consonant and the match will succeed. As a result, the rule as a whole has been matched with the letters in the word.

Consider another example with the following part of a word:

$$-TEALE-$$
$$\uparrow$$

Let the part of the rule being checked be as follows:

[A]!#:

The above rule applies to the letter 'A' and the symbols are to be checked against the letters following the letter 'A'. The letter 'L' would have to be checked against the symbol '!'. This matches, since the letter 'L' is a consonant. The next symbol to be checked is '#' against the letter 'E'. This again matches, since the letter 'E' is a vowel. More than one vowel has to be checked for, but in this case it would take us past the end of the word. However, the symbol has been correctly matched against the letter. The next symbol to be checked is ':' which corresponds to zero or more consonants. This again would match since zero consonants are present at the end of the word. The above rule-matching process as a whole has therefore been successful.

If at, any time, a symbol fails to match with the appropriate letter, then the matching process for that rule is abandoned and the next rule is considered. The points we have discussed so far have been implemented in the procedure 'searchformatch' and the function 'checkformatch.

A.2.4 Store phonemes into an array
Having obtained a matching rule, the next step is to make a copy of the phonemes generated by that rule in an array, building up the phonetic transcription as the word is scanned. This is accomplished by a call to the procedure 'putphoneme', which builds up the phonetically transcribed word.

Once a matching rule has been obtained, a value is taken from the rule record which indicates the number of letters to advance within the word being processed. The rules for the letter in this new position are then checked for an appropriate match. The whole process is repeated until the end of the word is encountered.

A.2.5 Display/file the phonemes of the word
The output from the program 'CONVERT' is two text files, namely 'moddic' and 'phondic'. The file 'moddic' contains both the original word and the phonetically transcribed word. The file 'phondic' only contains the phonetically transcribed word. Both files have been included but strictly speaking only the text file 'phondic' is necessary.

The only procedure which has not been mentioned so far is the procedure 'initialise', which performs all the usual initialisation of files, arrays, etc.

Finally, it is worthy of mention that besides being able to generate phonemes, we can equally generate codes which can subsequently be transmitted to a speech synthesiser.

A.3   THE PROGRAM 'CONVERT'

```
PROGRAM convert(INPUT,rulefile,moddic,phondic,OUTPUT);

CONST
      space          =   ' ';
      slash          =   '/';
      quote          =   '''';
      maxwordlen     =   23;
      maxphlen       =   60;
      maxsoundlen    =   12;
      backwards      =   -1;
      forwards       =   +1;

TYPE
      wordstore      = PACKED ARRAY [-1..maxwordlen] OF CHAR;
      phonemestore   = PACKED ARRAY [1..maxphlen] OF CHAR;
      rule1          = PACKED ARRAY [1..5] OF CHAR;
      rule2          = PACKED ARRAY [1..6] OF CHAR;
      soundtype      = PACKED ARRAY [1..maxsoundlen] OF CHAR;
      ptorulerec     = ^nextrecord;
      nextrecord     = RECORD
                           advance       : INTEGER;
                           preletterrule : rule1;
                           postletterrule : rule2;
                           sound         : soundtype;
                           rule          : INTEGER;
                           nextrule      : ptorulerec;
                       END;

      lpointers      = ARRAY ['A'..'Z'] OF ptorulerec;
      capitalset     = SET OF 'A'..'Z';

VAR
      capitals,                              { set of capital letters         }
      vowels,                                { set of vowels                  }
      vconsonants,                           { set of voiced consonants       }
      fvowels,                               { set of front vowels            }
      consonants     : capitalset;           { set of consonants              }
      table          : lpointers;            { table of rules; internal format }
      blankword,                             { blank word                     }
      neword         : wordstore;            { the word being pronounced      }
      newordlen,                             { the length of neword           }
      phlength,                              { the length of phword           }
      currentchar,                           { the current character position }
      count          : INTEGER;              { counter used in the main program }
      rulefile,                              { the file containing the rules  }
      moddic,                                { the file MODDIC                }
      phondic        : TEXT;                 { the file PHONDIC               }
      lastletter     : CHAR;                 { last letter read in            }
      blankphword,                           { blank for phword               }
      phword         : phonemestore;         { the phonemes for the word in neword }

      FUNCTION Apostrophe(letter : CHAR) : BOOLEAN;

      BEGIN
         Apostrophe := (lastletter IN capitals) AND
                       (letter = quote) AND (INPUT^ IN capitals)
      END;
```

Program CONVERT.

```
FUNCTION Letterok(letter : CHAR) : BOOLEAN;

BEGIN
   Letterok := (letter IN capitals)
END;


FUNCTION Letterinword(x : INTEGER) : CHAR;

BEGIN
   IF (x < 0) OR (x > maxwordlen) THEN
      Letterinword := '}'
   ELSE
      Letterinword := neword[x]
END;


PROCEDURE Makeupper(VAR letter : CHAR);

BEGIN
   IF (letter >= 'a') AND (letter <= 'z') THEN
      letter := CHR(ORD(letter) - 32)
END;


{PROCEDURE 'Insertintorule'

   This procedure reads in a line from the rules file, and stores it
internally. It is a simple insertion at the end of a  linked  list,
and is carried out cursively.
}

   PROCEDURE Insertintorule(VAR rulepointer : ptorulerec);

   VAR
      counter     : INTEGER;

   BEGIN
      IF (rulepointer <> NIL) THEN
         Insertintorule(rulepointer^.nextrule)   { find end of linked list }
      ELSE
      BEGIN
         NEW(rulepointer);                        { create new record }
         WITH rulepointer^ DO
         BEGIN
            READ(rulefile,advance);
            GET(rulefile);

            FOR counter := 5 DOWNTO 1 DO
               READ(rulefile,preletterrule[counter]);

            FOR counter := 1 TO 6 DO
               READ(rulefile,postletterrule[counter]);

            GET(rulefile);
            READ(rulefile,rule);

            GET(rulefile);
```

Program CONVERT.

```
        FOR counter := 1 TO maxsoundlen  DO
            READ(rulefile,sound[counter]);

        READLN(rulefile);
        nextrule := NIL;
      END
    END
  END; { PROCEDURE Insertintorule }
```

```
{PROCEDURE 'Readinnew'
```

   This procedure reads in the rules from the rules file and stores
them into the internally held rules table. As the rules in a block
apply to a single letter, all rules for each letter are read in and
stored in an array of linked lists, indexed by that letter.

   Procedure Insertintorule is used to read in each line from the
rules file, where each line of the file is a complete rule. The
rules file is sorted by rule letter. Each block of rules for a
given letter starts with that letter on a line by itself. A block
of rules is terminated by the digit '9' on a line by itself.
```
}
```

```
    PROCEDURE Readinnew;

    CONST
       terminator = '9';

    VAR
       currentletter    : CHAR;

    BEGIN
       RESET(rulefile);
       WHILE NOT EOF(rulefile) DO
       BEGIN
          READ(rulefile,currentletter);  { get letter for which the }
          READLN(rulefile);              { following rules apply.    }

          WHILE ((rulefile^ <> terminator) AND (NOT EOF)) DO
             Insertintorule(table[currentletter]);
          IF NOT EOF(rulefile) THEN
             READLN(rulefile)
       END
    END; { PROCEDURE Readinnew }
```

```
{PROCEDURE 'Readword'
```

   This procedure reads in the next word to be converted into
phonemes. Words longer than MAXWORDLEN characters are ignored.
```
}
```

```
    PROCEDURE Readword(VAR charcount : INTEGER);

    VAR
       letter    : CHAR;

       PROCEDURE Skiptospace(VAR infile : TEXT);
```

Program CONVERT.

```
{
    This procedure skips characters until the next space.
}
    BEGIN
       REPEAT
          READ(infile,letter);
          lastletter := letter;
       UNTIL letter = space;
    END; { PROCEDURE Skiptospace }
BEGIN
    charcount := 0;
    neword    := blankword;
    REPEAT
       READ(letter);
       Makeupper(letter);
       IF (Letterok(letter) OR Apostrophe(letter)) THEN
       BEGIN
          charcount := charcount + 1;
          IF (charcount <= maxwordlen) THEN
             neword[charcount] := letter
          ELSE
          BEGIN
             WRITE(' word greater than MAXWORDLEN chars found ');
             Skiptospace(INPUT);
          END;
          lastletter := letter;
       END;
       lastletter := letter;

    UNTIL NOT (Letterok(letter) OR Apostrophe(letter));
    lastletter := letter
END;


{FUNCTION 'Suffix'

   This function is used to  test  for  the  following  suffixes  to
words:
          E, ER, ES, ED, ING, ELY

   This assumes that a space indicates the end of a word.
}
    FUNCTION Suffix(w : INTEGER) : BOOLEAN;

    BEGIN
       Suffix := (
          ((Letterinword(w)   = 'E'  ) AND             { suffix E }
           (Letterinword(w+1) = space))
       OR
          ((Letterinword(w)   = 'E'  ) AND             { suffices ER, ES, ED }
           (Letterinword(w+1) in ['R','S','D'] ) AND
           (Letterinword(w+2) = space))
       OR
          ((Letterinword(w)   = 'I'  ) AND             { suffix ING }
           (Letterinword(w+1) = 'N'  ) AND
           (Letterinword(w+2) = 'G'  ) AND
           (Letterinword(w+3) = space))
       OR
          ((Letterinword(w)   = 'E'  ) AND             { suffix ELY }
```

Program CONVERT.

```
            (Letterinword(w+1) = 'L'  ) AND
            (Letterinword(w+2) = 'Y'  ) AND
            (Letterinword(w+3) = space))
      )
   END;
```

```
{FUNCTION 'Checkformatch'
```

This checks a special symbol from a rule against the actual word,
to see if it matches. The use of the parameter 'adv' allows searching
both backwards and forwards along the word.
```
}
   FUNCTION Checkformatch(adv          : INTEGER;
                          cha          : CHAR;
                     var position      : INTEGER) : BOOLEAN;

   VAR
      gotamatch : BOOLEAN;

   BEGIN
      gotamatch := FALSE;
      CASE cha OF

         '#': IF Letterinword(position) IN vowels THEN BEGIN
                 WHILE (Letterinword(position) IN vowels) DO
                 BEGIN
                    gotamatch := TRUE;
                    position := position + adv
                 END;
                 position := position - adv
              END;

         '.': gotamatch := (Letterinword(position) IN vconsonants);

         '%': gotamatch := Suffix(position);

         '&': IF (Letterinword(position) IN ['S','C','Z','X','J']) THEN
                 gotamatch := TRUE
              ELSE
                 IF (Letterinword(position)    = 'H') AND
                    (Letterinword(position - 1) IN ['C','S']) THEN
                 BEGIN
                    gotamatch := TRUE;
                    position := position - 1;
                 END;

         '?': IF (Letterinword(position) IN
                    ['D','J','L','N','R','S','T','Z']) THEN
                 gotamatch := TRUE
              ELSE
                 IF (Letterinword(position) = 'H') AND
                    (Letterinword(position - 1) IN ['S','T']) THEN
                 BEGIN
                    gotamatch := TRUE;
                    position := position - 1;
                 END;

         '!': IF Letterinword(position) IN consonants THEN
```

Program CONVERT.

```
                        gotamatch := TRUE;

        '+': IF Letterinword(position) IN fvowels THEN
                gotamatch := TRUE;

        ':': BEGIN
                gotamatch := TRUE;
                IF Letterinword(position) IN consonants THEN
                  BEGIN
                    WHILE (Letterinword(position) IN consonants) DO
                      position := position + adv;
                      position := position - adv
                  END
                ELSE position := position - adv;
             END;

        '$': IF Letterinword(position) = space THEN
                gotamatch := TRUE;

    END;
    Checkformatch := gotamatch
  END; { FUNCTION Checkformatch }


{PROCEDURE 'Putphoneme'

   This puts a phoneme, as found in a rule, into the  string  phword.
 The variable phlength gives the length of phword, and is incremented
 accordingly.
}
  PROCEDURE Putphoneme (sound : soundtype) ;

  VAR
     first,
     last,
     count  : INTEGER;

  BEGIN
     count := maxsoundlen;
     WHILE (sound[count]=space) and (count>1) DO
        count := count - 1;
     IF (sound[count]=slash) THEN
     BEGIN
        first := 2;
        last := count - 1
     END
     ELSE
     BEGIN
        first := 1;
        last := count
     END;
     FOR count := first TO last DO
        phword[phlength+count-first+1] := sound[count];
     phlength := phlength + last - first + 2;
     phword[phlength] := slash
  END;


{PROCEDURE 'Searchformatch' }
```

Program CONVERT.

```
    PROCEDURE Searchformatch(thisrule : ptorulerec);

{ The following three variables are used to keep track of the letters
  and symbols under consideration.
}
    VAR
        charptr,
        postpos,
        prepos     : INTEGER;
        matchfound : BOOLEAN;

    BEGIN
        WITH thisrule^ DO BEGIN

{ First, check the pre-letter rule for a possible match.
}
            matchfound := TRUE;
            prepos  := 1;
            charptr := currentchar;
            REPEAT
                IF (preletterrule[prepos] <> space) THEN
                BEGIN
                    charptr := charptr - 1;
                    IF Letterok(preletterrule[prepos]) OR
                        (preletterrule[prepos] = quote) THEN
                    BEGIN
                        IF (preletterrule[prepos]<>Letterinword(charptr)) THEN
                            matchfound := FALSE
                    END
                    ELSE
                        matchfound := Checkformatch(backwards,
                                                    preletterrule[prepos],
                                                    charptr);
                    IF matchfound THEN
                        prepos := prepos + 1
                END
            UNTIL (preletterrule[prepos] = space) OR
                NOT matchfound OR (prepos = 5);

{ Now, if the pre-letter rule matches, then check  the  post-letter
  rule.
}
            IF matchfound THEN BEGIN
                postpos  := 1;
                charptr := currentchar;
                REPEAT
                    IF (postletterrule[postpos] <> space) THEN
                    BEGIN
                        charptr := charptr + 1;
                        IF Letterok(postletterrule[postpos]) OR
                            (postletterrule[postpos] = quote) THEN
                        BEGIN
                            IF (postletterrule[postpos]<>Letterinword(charptr)) THEN
                                matchfound := FALSE
                        END
                        ELSE
                            matchfound := Checkformatch(forwards,
                                                        postletterrule[postpos],
```

Program CONVERT.

```
                                                   charptr);
                        IF matchfound THEN
                           postpos := postpos + 1
                     END
                  UNTIL (postletterrule[postpos] = space) OR
                        NOT matchfound OR (postpos = 6)
            END;
            IF matchfound THEN
            BEGIN
               Putphoneme(sound);
               currentchar := currentchar + advance
            END
            ELSE
               Searchformatch(nextrule);
         END
      END; { PROCEDURE Searchformatch }


{PROCEDURE 'Initialise'}

   PROCEDURE Initialise;

   VAR
      ch : CHAR;
      count : INTEGER;

   BEGIN
      capitals     := ['A'..'Z'];
      vowels       := ['A', 'E', 'I', 'O', 'U', 'Y'];
      vconsonants  := ['B', 'D', 'V', 'G', 'J', 'L', 'M', 'N', 'R', 'W', 'Z'];
      fvowels      := ['E', 'I', 'Y'];
      consonants   := ['B', 'C', 'D', 'F', 'G', 'H', 'J', 'K', 'L', 'M', 'N',
                       'P','Q','R', 'S', 'T', 'V', 'W', 'X', 'Z'];

      FOR ch := 'A' TO 'Z' DO
         table[ch] := NIL;
      REWRITE(moddic);
      REWRITE(phondic);
      Readinnew;
      lastletter := space;
      FOR count := -1 TO maxwordlen DO
         blankword[count] := space;
      FOR count := 1 TO maxphlen DO
         blankphword[count] := space
   END; { PROCEDURE Initialise }


{MAIN PROGRAM}

BEGIN
   Initialise;
   WHILE NOT EOF DO
   BEGIN
      Readword(newordlen);
      IF (newordlen>=1) THEN
      BEGIN
         currentchar := 1;
         phlength    := 0;
         phword      := blankphword;
```

Program CONVERT.

```
            WHILE (currentchar<=newordlen) DO
            BEGIN
               IF (neword[currentchar] = quote) THEN
                  currentchar := currentchar + 1
               ELSE
                  Searchformatch(table[neword[currentchar]])
            END;
            FOR count := 1 TO maxwordlen DO
               WRITE(moddic,neword[count],space);
            WRITELN(moddic,slash,phword);
            WRITELN(phondic,slash,phword);
         END;
      END;
END.
```

Program CONVERT.

A.4   RULES FOR LETTER-TO-PHONEME TRANSFORMATIONS

The rules applying to each letter appear in a block where the letter itself signifies the beginning of the block and number '9' the end. Within each block, the format is as follows:

(a)   The number in the first column indicates the advance forward while scanning a word.

(b)   The next positions (maximum 11) contain symbols and letters which have to be matched against the letters in a word under analysis. The notation we adopt here is presented in Table A.1. Note that, if all 11 positions are blank, then a default phoneme is generated.

(c)   The next position holds an identification number (1 to 308).

(d)   Next, there are the phonemes in slashes (//) where a space separates the individual phonemes.

(e)   Finally, the full stop serves as a simple end of record marker.

Table A.1 — Definition of the symbols used in program 'CONVERT'

Symbol	Definition
#	One or more vowels
·	A voiced consonant
%	A suffix
&	One of (S, C, Z, X, J, CH, SH)
?	One of (D, J, L, N, R, S, T, Z, SH, TH)
!	A consonant
+	A front vowel
:	Zero or more consonants
$	A space

Where	
Vowels	= [A, E, I, O, U, Y]
Voiced consonants	= [B, D, V, G, J, L, M, N, R, W, Z]
Front vowels	= [E, I, Y]
Consonants	= [B, C, D, F, G, H, J, K, L, M, N, P, Q, R, S, T, V, W, X, Z]
Suffix	= [E, ER, ES, ED, ING, ELY]

A.4.1   Rules and associated phonemes

A

1	$	1 /ax/ .
3	RE	2 /aa r/ .
2	$RO	3 /ax r/ .
2	R#	4 /eh r/ .
2	!S#	5 /ey s/ .
1	WA	6 /ax/ .
2	W	7 /ao/ .
3	$:NY	8 /eh n iy/ .
1	!+#	9 /ey/ .
4	#:LLY	10 /ax l iy/ .
2	$L#	11 /ax l/ .
5	GAIN	12 /ax g eh n/ .
2	#:GE	13 /ih jh/ .
1	!+:#	14 /ae/ .
1	$:!+$	15 /ey/ .
1	!%	16 /ey/ .
3	$RR	17 /ax r/ .
3	RR	18 /ae r/ .
2	$:R$	19 /aa r/ .
2	R$	20 /er/ .
2	R	21 /aa r/ .
3	IR	22 /eh r/ .
2	I	23 /ey/ .
2	Y	24 /ey/ .
2	U	25 /ao/ .
2	#:L$	26 /ax l/ .
3	#:LS$	27 /ax l z/ .
3	LK	28 /ao k/ .
2	L!	29 /ao l/ .
4	$:BLE	30 /ey b ax l/ .
4	BLE	31 /ax b ax l/ .
3	NG+	32 /ey n jh/ .
1		33 /ae/ .
9		

B

2	$E!#	34 /b ih/ .
5	EING	35 /b iy ih nx/ .
4	OTH	36 /b ow th/ .
3	$US#	37 /b ih z/ .
4	UIL	38 /b ih l/ .
1		39 /b/ .
9		

C

2	$H!	40 /k/ .
2	!EH	41 /k/ .
2	H	42 /ch/ .

3	#:LY$	80 /l iy/	.
5	#:MENT	81 /m eh n t/	.
4	FUL	82 /f uh l/	.
2	E	83 /iy/	.
4	ARN	84 /er n/	.
3	$AR!	85 /er/	.
2	$SI#	43 /s ay/	.
2	IA	44 /sh/	.
2	IO	45 /sh/	.
2	IEN	46 /sh/	.
1	+	47 /s/	.
2	K	48 /k/	.
3	OM%	49 /k ah m/	.
1		50 /k/	.
9			
D			
3	#:ED$	51 /d ih d/	.
1	.E$	52 /d/	.
1	#!:E$	53 /t/	.
2	$E!#	54 /d ih/	.
2	O	55 /d uw/	.
4	$OES	56 /d ah z/	.
5	$OING	57 /d uw ih nx/	.
3	$OW	58 /d aw/	.
2	UA	59 /jh uw/	.
1		60 /d/	.
9			
E			
1	#:$	61 / /	.
1	':$	62 / /	.
1	$:$	63 /iy/	.
2	#D$	64 /d/	.
1	#:D$	65 / /	.
2	VER	66 /eh v/	.
1	!%	67 /iy/	.
3	RI#	68 /iy r iy/	.
3	RI	69 /eh r ih/	.
2	#:R#	70 /er/	.
2	R#	71 /eh r/	.
2	R	72 /er/	.
4	$VEN	73 /iy v eh n/	.
1	#:W	74 / /	.
2	?W	75 /uw/	.
2	W	76 /y uw/	.
2	O	77 /iy/	.
2	#:&S$	78 /ih z/	.
1	#:S$	79 / /	.

3	AD	86 /eh d/	.
2	#:A$	87 /iy ax/	.
2	ASU	88 /eh/	.
2	A	89 /iy/	.
4	IGH	90 /ey/	.
2	I	91 /iy/	.
3	$YE	92 /ay/	.
2	Y	93 /iy/	.
2	U	94 /y uw/	.
1		95 /eh/	.
9			
F			
3	UL	96 /f uh l/	.
1		97 /f/	.
9			
G			
3	IV	98 /g ih v/	.
1	$I!	99 /g/	.
2	ET	100 /g eh/	.
4	SUGES	101 /g jh eh s/	.
2	G	102 /g/	.
1	$B#	103 /g/	.
1	+	104 /jh/	.
5	REAT	105 /g r ey t/	.
2	#H	106 / /	.
1		107 /g/	.
9			
H			
3	$AV	108 /hh ae v/	.
4	$ERE	109 /hh iy r/	.
4	$OUR	110 /aw er/	.
3	OW	111 /hh aw/	.
1	#	112 /hh/	.
1		113 / /	.
9			
I			
2	$N	114 /ih n/	.
1	$$	115 /ay/	.
2	ND	116 /ay n/	.
3	ER	117 /iy er/	.
3	#:REDS	118 /iy d/	.
3	ED$	119 /ay d/	.
3	EN	120 /iy eh n/	.
2	ET	121 /ay eh/	.
1	$:%	122 /ay/	.
1	%	123 /iy/	.
2	E	124 /iy/	.

1	!+:#	125 /ih/	.
2	R#	126 /ay r/	.
2	Z%	127 /ay z/	.
2	S%	128 /ay z/	.
1	D%	129 /ay/	.
1	+!!+	130 /ih/	.
1	T%	131 /ay/	.
1	#:!+	132 /ih	.
1	!+	133 /ay/	.
2	R	134 /er/	.
3	GH	135 /ay/	.
3	LD	136 /ay l d/	.
3	GN!	137 /ay n/	.
3	GN$	138 /ay n/	.
3	GN%	139 /ay n/	.
4	QUE	140 /iy k/	.
1		141 /ih/	.
9			
J			
1		142 /jh/	.
9			
K			
1	$N	143 / /	.
1		144 /k/	.
9			
L			
2	OC#	145 /l ow/	.
1	L	146 / /	.
1	#:%	147 /ax l/	.
4	EAD	148 /l iy d/	.
1		149 /l/	.
9			
M			
3	OV	150 /m uw v/	.
1		151/m/	.
9			
N			
2	EG+	152 /n jh/	.
2	GR	153 /nx g/	.
2	G#	154 /nx g/	.
3	GL%	155 /nx g ax l/	.
2	G	156 /nx/	.
2	K	157 /nx k/	.
3	OW	158 /n aw/	.
1		159 /n/	.
9			

O

2	F$	160 /ax v/
6	ROUGH	161 /er ow/
2	#:R$	162 /er/
3	#:RS$	163 /er z/
2	R	164 /ao r/
3	$NE	165 /w ah n/
2	W	166 /ow/
4	$VER	167 /ow v er/
2	V	168 /ah v/
1	!%	169 /ow/
1	!EN	170 /ow/
1	!I#	171 /ow/
2	LD	172 /ow l/
5	UGHT	173 /ao t/
4	UGH	174 /ah f/
2	$U	175 /aw/
2	HUS#	176 /aw/
3	US	177 /ax s/
3	UR	178 /ao r/
4	ULD	179 /uh d/
2	U!L	180 /ah/
3	UP	181 /uw p/
2	U	182 /aw/
2	Y	183 /oy/
4	ING	184 /ow ih nx/
2	I	185 /oy/
3	OR	186 /ao r/
3	OK	187 /uh k/
3	OD	188 /uh d/
2	O	189 /uw/
1	E	190 /ow/
1	$	191 /ow/
2	A	192 /ow/
4	$NLY	193 /ow n l iy/
4	$NCE	194 /w ah n s/
4	N'T	195 /ow n t/
1	CN	196 /aa/
1	NG	197 /ao/
2	IN	198 /ax n/
2	#:N$	199 /ax n/
2	#!N	200 /ax n/
1	:N	201 /ah/
1	ST$	202 /ow/
2	F!	203 /ao f/
5	THER	204 /ah dh er/
3	SS$	205 /ao s/

2	#:M	206 /ah m/	.
1		207 /aa/	.
9			
P			
2	H	208 /f/	.
4	EOP	209 /p iy p/	.
3	OW	210 /p aw/	.
3	UT$	211 /p uh t/	.
1		212 /p/	.
9			
Q			
4	UAR	213 /k w ao r/	.
2	U	214 /k w/	.
1		215 /k/	.
9			
R			
2	E!#	216 /r iy/	.
1		217 /r/	.
9			
S			
2	H	218 /sh/	.
4	#ION	219 /zh ax n/	.
4	OME	220 /s ah m/	.
3	#UR#	221 /zh er/	.
3	UR#	222 /sh er/	.
2	#U#	223 /zh uw/	.
3	#SU#	224 /sh uw/	.
3	#ED$	225 /z d/	.
1	##	226 /z/	.
4	AID	227 /s eh d/	.
4	!ION	228 /sh ax n/	.
1	S	229 / /	.
1	.$	230 /z/	.
1	#:.E$	231 /z/	.
1	#:##$	232 /z/	.
1	#:#$	233 /s/	.
1	U$	234 /s/	.
1	$:#$	235 /z/	.
3	$CH	236 /s k/	.
1	C+	237 / /	.
2	#M	238 /z m/	.
2	#N'	239 /z ax n/	.
1		240 /s/	.
9			
T			
3	HE	241 /dh ax/	.
2	O$	242 /t uw/	.

4	HAT$	243 /dh ae t/	.
4	HIS	244 /dh ih s/	.
4	$HEY	245 /dh ey/	.
5	$HERE	246 /dh eh r/	.
4	HER	247 /dh er/	.
5	HEIR	248 /dh eh r/	.
4	HAN	249 /dh ae n/	.
4	HEM	250 /dh eh m/	.
5	HESE$	251 /dh iy z/	.
4	$HEN	252 /dh eh n/	.
7	HROUGH	253 /th r uw/	.
5	HOSE	254 /dh ow z/	.
6	HOUGH$	255 /dh ow/	.
4	$HUS	256 /dh ah s/	.
2	H	257 /th/	.
3	#:ED$	258 /t ih d/	.
2	SI#N	259 /ch/	.
2	IO	260 /sh/	.
2	IA	261 /sh/	.
4	IEN	262 /sh ax n/	.
3	UR#	263 /ch er/	.
2	UA	264 /ch uw/	.
3	$WO	265 /t uw/	.
1		266 /t/	.
9			
U			
2	$NI	267 /y uw n/	.
2	$N	268 /ah n/	.
4	$PON	269 /ax p ao n /	.
2	?R#	270 /uh r/	.
2	R#	271 /y uh r/	.
2	R	272 /er/	.
1	!$	273 /ah/	.
1	!!	274 /ah/	.
2	Y	275 /ay/	.
1	$G#	276 / /	.
1	G%	277 / /	.
1	G#	278 /w/	.
1	#N	279 /y uw/	.
1	?	280 /uw/	.
1		281 /y uw/	.
9			
V			
4	IEW	282 /v y uw/	.
1		283 /v/	.

9			
W			
4	$ERE	284 /w er/	.
2	AS	285 /w aa/	.
2	AT	286 /w aa/	.
5	HERE	287 /wh eh r/	.
4	HAT	288 /wh aa t/	.
4	HOL	289 /hh ow l/	.
3	HO	290 /hh uw/	.
2	H	291 /wh/	.
3	AR	292 /w ao r/	.
3	OR!	293 /w er/	.
2	R	294 /r/	.
1		295 /w/	.
9			
X			
1		296 /k s/	.
9			
Y			
5	OUNG	297 /y ah nx/	.
3	$OU	298 /y uw/	.
3	$ES	299 /y eh s/	.
1	$	300 /y/	.
1	#:$	301 /iy/	.
1	#:I	302 /iy/	.
1	$:$	303 /ay/	.
1	$:#	304 /ay/	.
1	$:!+:#	305 /ih/	.
1	:!#	306 /ay/	.
1		307 /ih/	.
9			
Z			
1		308 /z/	.
9			

APPENDIX B: An example V.P.L. program

This appendix presents an example program written in V.P.L., for a three-person message centre. The source code contains ample comments for the reader to follow the logic behind this application.

```
!VPL-PC Example
! Three Mailbox Message Centre.
! Host is keyboard/display of the computer.
!
! Exclamation characters (!) in column 1 indicate a comment line.
! Hash signs (#) in column 1 indicate definition-statements
! similar to declarations of variables in other languages.
#def dialog exple
#def template onee
#text           onee      comm="box1"
#def template   twoo
#text           twoo      comm="box2"
#def template   threee
#text           threee    comm="box3"
#def template   yess
#text           yess      response="y"
#def template   noo
#text           noo       response="n"
#def template   sendd
#text           sendd     comm="se"
#def template   receivee
#text           receivee  comm="re"
!
! The prompt string associated with each message indicates what
! voice response goes with each message variable.
! These prompt strings are designed to aid the programmer.
! They have no effect on program compilation or execution
! and are completely optional.
! A recording of each message must be made (using BLD)
! before the program is executed.
```

!
#def message	repeatme		
#text	repeatme	prompt =	"Please repeat each word I say. Wait for the tone each time."
#def message	timee		
#text	timee	prompt =	"Time out."
#def message	repeat		
#text	repeat	prompt =	"Please repeat."
#def message	box1		
#text	box1	prompt =	"The box is empty."
#def message	box2		
#text	box2	prompt =	"The box is empty."
#def message	box3		
#text	box3	prompt =	"The box is empty."
#def message	spkclr		
#text	spkclr	prompt =	"Did you say each word clearly?"
#def message	qfcn		

!
! Emphasise the word "sendd" and "receivee" in the string below
!
#text	qfcn	prompt =	"Would you like to send or receive a message?"
#def message	qbox		
#text	qbox	prompt =	"Which box do you wish? One, Two or Three."
#def message	startrec		
#text	startrec	prompt =	"Start recording your message at the tone."
#def message	qagain	prompt =	"Do you have another transaction
#text	qagain		
#def message	instruct		
#text	instruct	prompt =	"Welcome to the Message Centre."
#def message	gbye		
#text	gbye	prompt =	"Thank you for using the Message Centre."

!
! Each message starting with "m" is one-word voice response message
! used to prompt users during training. This convention is not
! mandatory.
! Note that no prompts were assigned to the messages below.
! Prompts are always optional.
!
| #def message | myess | | |

```
#text              myessm prompt = "yes"
#def message       mnoo
#text              mnoo prompt = "no"
#def message       monee
#text              monee prompt = "one"
#def message       mtwo
#text              mtwoo prompt = "two"
#def message       mthree
#text              mthree prompt = "three"
#def message       msendd
#text              msendd prompt = "send"
#def message       mreceive
#text              mreceive prompt = "receive"
!
! Define sub-sets of the entire vocabulary and assign them names
#def    set yessnoo     yess, noo
#def    set boxno       onee, twoo, threee
#def    set getorput    sendd, receivee
!
! Initialise
!          clear V.P.L.'s built-in soft buffers
           clear comm
           clear resp
           clear b1
           clear b2
           clear b3
           clear b4
!                                    Restore voice data from file
                                     restore messages from exple
!
! Begin the demonstration
5:         call 130:
!          Wait until user starts demo using computer keyboard control
           call 300:
           say instruct
!
! Ask the user to say each word to be recognised
10:        say repeatme
           train yess       prompt=myess
           train noo        prompt=mnoo
           train onee       prompt=monee
           train twoo       prompt=mtwoo
           train threee     prompt=mthreee
           train sendd      prompt=msendd
           train receivee   prompt=mreceivee
!
```

```
!          Ask user if each word was said clearly during training recognize
           yessnoo prompt=spkclr
!          If the user says anything other than "yes"
!          erase all templates and train again.
           if resp ne "y"
                     call 130:
                     goto 10:
           endif
!
15:        clear comm
!
! Ask if the user wants to send or receive a message
20:        recognize getorput prompt=qfcn
!          Check for "time out" or "no match" conditions
           call 200:
!          If error code is returned, ignore user's last input
           if b4 eq "err"
                     clear b4
                     goto 20:
           endif
!
! Ask which mailbox the user wishes to use
30:        recognize boxno prompt=qbox
           call 200
!          if error code is returned, ignore user's last input
!          and re-prompt for input
           if b4 eq "err"
                     clear b4
                     goto 30:
           endif
!
! Show the contents of the communications buffer on the VDU.
! Characters 1 and 2 contain the code for "send" or "receive".
! Characters 3, 4, 5, and 6 contain the code for the box number.
! For example, if the user wishes to send a message to
! box 3, the communications buffer will contain "sebox3"
!
! Display the contents of the comm buffer on the computer screen
           show comm
!
! Put the code for the box number into buffer 1
           move comm(3,4) to b1
!
! Send or receive a message for each user request.
! Decode user request using the first two characters of comm buffer
  if comm(1,2) eq "re"
```

```
                    say b1
          elseif comm(1,2) eq "se"
                    record b1 prompt=startrec
          endif
!
! Ask if the user has another transaction
40:       recognize yessnoo prompt=qagain
          call 200:
!          if error code is returned, ignore user's last input
!          and re-prompt for input
          if b4 eq "err"
                    clear b4
                    goto 40:
          elseif resp eq "n"
                    say gbye
                    goto 5:
          elseif resp eq "y"
                    goto 15:"
          endif
!
!
! Check for time out and no match conditions, return error code in b4
200:      if timedout
                    say timee
                    move "err" to b4
          elseif nomatch
                    say repeat
                    move "err" to b4
          endif
          return
!
! Allow user to control start of demo from keyboard.
! Carriage return and line feed are implemented via decimal
! ASCII equivalent.
300:      move <10><13> "The Message Centre is Ready"<10><13>
to comm
!          Display the contents of the comm buffer on the computer display.
!          The 'tohost' statement is equivalent to 'show comm' in this
!          program because the host is the computer keyboard/display.
          tohost
          move <10><13><10><13> "This is a demonstration of a three
                    mail-box bulletin board" to comm
          tohost
          move <10><13> "You will be asked to repeat several words to
                    control the bulletin" to comm
          tohost
          move <10><13> "board. Then, you will be able to send or
```

```
            receive messages to or from" to comm
        tohost
        move <10><13> "any one of three mail boxes under voice
        control." to comm
        tohost
        move <10><13><10><13> "Strike 'carriage return' to begin"
                <10><13> to comm
        tohost
        clear comm
        fromhost
        clear comm
        return
!
! Clear templates for new user
130:    delete onee
        delete twoo
        delete threee
        delete yess
        delete noo
        delete sendd
        delete receivee
        return
```

APPENDIX C: V.P.L. Reserved Words

The following words are reserved for V.P.L; avoid using these for dialogue names or elements.

ACCEPT	ENDDO	RESP
ANSWER	EXECUTE	RESPONSE
APPEND	EXIT	RESTORE
B1	FEEDBACK	RETURN
B2	FROMHOST	ROTARY
B3	GAIN	SAVE
B4	GAININ	SAY
B5	GAINOUT	SEND
B6	GOTO	SET
B7	HOST	SHOW
B8	ISOLATED	SOURCE
BITRATE	LOAD	SRL
BUSY	MESSAGE	TBUF
CALL	MOVE	TEMPLATE
CLEAR	NODIAL	TERM
CLEARLAST	NOMATCH	TEXT
COMM	NONE	TIME
CONTINUOUS	NOT	TIMEDOUT
COUNT	NOT.OK	TIMES
D1	OFF	TOHOST
D2	OFFHOOK	TONEBUF
DEF	ON	TONEIN
DELAY	ONHOOK	TONEOUT
DELETE	PARS	TRAIN
DEST	PART	TURN
DIAL	PHONE	TWAIT
DIALOG	PROG	VINT
DIGITS	PROMPT	VOCODE
DO	RECEIVE	W1
ELSE	RECOGNIZE	W2
ELSEIF	RECORD	WHILE

Glossary of speech synthesis and recognition terms

Acoustic ratio: This is the ratio between the intensity of the source (e.g. human voice) and the intensity of the signals encapsulated by the voice recognition device. It depends on the distance between the voice source and the device, the polar distribution of the incoming signals, and the period of reverberation at the device accepting the signals.

Adaptive delta modulation (A.D.M.): A technique for digitising speech signals, similar to A.D.P.C.M., but where only a 1-bit quantiser is used. This technique is normally used with rather low bit rate digitisation environments. Single chips which adopt A.D.M. are available.

Adaptive differential pulse code modulation (A.D.P.C.M.): A technique for digitising speech signals, similar to pulse code modulation, but where the quantiser adapts itself to the difference signal and can therefore employ a variable number of bits. The principle behind A.D.P.C.M. is that an incoming signal can be 'predicted' by keeping track of immediately preceding samples. The same principle is used in the technique of linear predictive coding of speech.

Affricative: A sequence of stop and fricative consonants which realises a single phoneme; for example "ts".

Allophone: A variant of a phoneme which characterises its precise nature within a given context. Note that a phoneme may have one or more allophones, depending on the context(s) in which these occur. The actual allophonic sound produced is based on a set of rules which analyse the environment of a phoneme. Allophonic rules therefore aim to identify the correct sound(s) for specific contexts.

Amplitude: This is the maximum displacement from the point of rest, for a molecule undergoing vibration.

Bandwidth: A very important parameter in speech synthesis and recognition systems is the bandwidth, in other words, the frequency range of speech. For high-fidelity speech, approximately 20 kHz is appropriate, although with present-day speech-processing systems a bandwidth of between approximately 4 and 5 kHz is often enforced. This is found to be a reasonable compromise between data rate (bits per second of speech) and quality of speech.

Channel coding: A technique for digitising speech signals, similar to formant coding, but where the encoder divides the source signals into bands of frequencies irrespective of where the actual formants occur. This is achieved by employing a set of filters in parallel, each processing the amplitude of its associated frequency band, and a technique for determining whether a sound is voiced or not.

Co-articulation: The merging or overlapping of two adjacent 'sounds'. Co-articulation occurs because the tongue, lips, jaws, etc., cannot leap from one target position to the next but performs a blending process which gives rise to a smooth and continuous flow.

Cycle: For sound, one cycle is the movement from the point of rest, to the maximum displacement at one side, to the maximum displacement at the other, and finally back to the point of rest, for a molecule undergoing vibration.

Cycle period: The length of time it takes to complete one cycle.

Data commpression techniques: These techniques all involve the minimisation of the amount of the transmitted/stored data. An example compression method is based on predicting the value of the next sample(s) from the current sample(s).

Data rate (speed): The rate at which digital information is encoded/ decoded during its transmission over the communications channel. It can be measured in bits or bytes per second.

Differential pulse code modulation (D.P.C.M.): The difference between the incoming and the predicted sample is quantised in steps of amplitude and encoded for transmission. The predictor algorithm generally requires knowledge of the signal and the technique is therefore signal-specific.

Digital Storage: A general term used when an analogue signal has been sampled and then stored as a series of digits. When storing speech signals we aim to take sufficient samples so that the reconstructed signal will be indistinguishable from the real signal, while at the same time minimising the number of samples stored.

Formant: Peaks in the energy spectrum of the speech wave are known as formants. They arise when the position of the vocal organs remains static, as a result of which the vocal tract resonates at three or four overtone frequencies which are determined by the characteristics of the vocal tract. A formant is normally represented by a dark band on a spectrograph.

Formant coding: A technique for digitising speech following spectral analysis of the speech signal. The technique of formant coding requires substantial computing time and therefore it becomes impractical for use in real-time voice-processing environments.

Glottis: The gap between the vocal cords. The closure of this gap can be utilised to stop the flow of air from the lungs; pressure then builds up until it is released explosively. The sound produced by this process is known as a 'glottal stop'.

Interpolators: These utilise knowledge of both past and future samples in their predictor algorithms.

Intonation: This is defined as the 'modulation of the voice in speaking', and is produced by the variations in the rate of vibration of the vocal cords (i.e. the pitch).

Linear predictive coding (L.P.C.): This technique of coding speech signals utilises linear prediction as a filter to determine and to store incoming signals, whereas formant encoding utilises the filter to approximate the formant frequencies of a sound. The principle behind L.P.C. is that incoming signals can be predicted by a linear combination of the most recent speech samples. The basic components of an L.P.C. synthesiser are: (a) the switch which selects the pulse/noise source–the pulse produces the voiced signals and the noise source produces the fricative signals; (b) the gain control which looks after the amplitude of the source; and (c) the linear predictor which manipulates the so-called 'predictor coefficients' using numerical analysis techniques (e.g. Fourier analysis).

Morph: The spelling representation of an abstract morpheme.

Morpheme: A distinguishable and meaningful linguistic form which is different from others with similar sounds. A morpheme is not usually divided into other forms. For example, the word 'national' consists of the morphemes 'nation' and 'al'.

n-gram: One or more consecutive letters as they occur naturally in text. For example, the word HELLO contains: four bi-grams (HE, EL, LL and LO), three trigrams (HEL, ELL, and LLO), and two tetragrams (HELL and ELLO). Clearly, the only pentagram is the complete word itself. The range of *n* depends on the application, the maximum word length used, the number of words analysed, the number of different *n*-grams required, etc.

Nasal: A sound produced when the air passage through the nose is open is known as a 'nasal sound'.

Obstruent: A term used to distinguish consonants which require a considerable degree of obstruction from those only requiring a limited amount of obstruction. Stops, fricatives and affricatives are therefore all obstruents.

Parametric coding: Coding techniques which utilise knowledge of the speech process. Certain parameters are extracted from the signal prior to digitisation, and are then coded separately.

Periodic sounds: These are sounds whose period remains the same cycle after cycle.

Phone: The smallest component of speech which forms a distinctive (identifiable) sound. (See also 'Allophone').

Phoneme: This is the logical representation of the phones present in speech and is an organisational convenience used to group the distinctive speech sounds. A number of phonemes constitute a morpheme, or a word, or an acceptable utterance. Each phoneme is usually denoted by a combination of letters/symbols enclosed in slashes ('/'). Take for example the following phonemes and corresponding words:

/f/   *f*ight
/z/   *z*eal
/m/   ja*m*
/dʒ/   bri*dge*

Phonology: The study of the structure, organisation, changes, and transformations of speech sounds with reference to particular languages or dialects. Also the generation, representation in coded form and classification of speech sounds.

Phonotactics: A term used to refer to the way the phonemes of a particular language are allowed to combine together. For example, two languages might utilise the same phonemes but these phonemes would not necessarily combine together in the same way. Thus, it is not sufficient merely to list the phonemes of a language in order to describe that language.

Plosive: A term used to describe a speech sound which is produced by the explosive or sudden release of air. This can be accomplished either with or without voicing.

Polyphone: A written letter, word or syllable which maps onto a different phoneme in different words or contexts. The phoneme thus depends on the surrounding units and can be established by following a set of rules. See also 'Allophone'.

Predictors: These utilise knowledge of past samples in their predicting algorithms.

Pulse code modulation (P.C.M.): A technique for digitising signals where information is quantised and coded with respect to the time interval. The signal is first filtered to a bandwidth of approximately 4 kHz and then sampled at approximately 8 kHz, in order to limit its highest frequency.

Quantisation: A technique for dividing the amplitude of a wave into a number of sub-ranges which are restricted, that is, a finite number of amplitudes. Quantisation of amplitude is caused by using an analogue-to-digital converter (A.D.C.) with its limited resolution. For example, an 8-bit A.D.C. can convert an incoming signal into one of 256 levels. Noise, as a result of quantisation, can be reduced by increasing the resolution of the A.D.C. to, say, at least 10 bits, giving a resolution of one part in 1024.

Sonorant: A term used to distinguish consonants which require a limited amount of obstruction from those requiring a considerable amount of obstruction. An example of a sonorant sound is /w/.

Sound: For our purposes here, a sound is a human utterance which can be represented by the position of its formants, the amplitude and the pitch period of the excitation. Sounds can be analysed with a spectrograph.

Spectrograph: An instrument used to analyse sound signals into their various wavelength components. It comprises a slit and collimator in order to produce beams of radiation in parallel, a prism in order to distribute different wavelengths through different angles and therefore deviate the beams, and a telescope which enables us to observe the distribution of the beams. A spectrograph usually enables the analysis and photographic recording of a wide range of frequencies.

Speech quality: A measure of how well encoding/reproduction captures the natural characteristics of the human voice. In order to generate high-quality speech, the signals reproduced must be as close as possible to the human voice.

Stress: This term is used to describe the stronger muscular effort, both articulatory and respiratory, we feel in connection with some syllables in the English language.

Suprasegmental features: This term is used to refer to the extra information conveyed by how we say things, that is, the information conveyed on top of the the actual words spoken.

Transeme: This term is used to represent a vowel–consonant sequence such that the segment extends from the centre of the vowel to the centre of the consonant and vice versa.

Voicing: Speech sounds can be produced either with or without the vocal cords vibrating. When speech sounds are produced with the vocal cords vibrating they are known as 'voiced sounds', whereas, those produced without the vocal cords vibrating are known as 'voiceless sounds.

Waveform coding: Sometimes referred to as 'time waveform coding'. In this class of coding techniques the signal is sampled and subsequently digitised as a function of time.

References and bibliography

Allen, J. (1983) 'VLSI Applications: Speech Processing', In *The Fifth Generation Computer Project: State of the Art Report*, Scarrot, G. G. (editor), Pergamon Infotech, pp. 41–48.

Allen, J., Carlson, B., Grandstrom, B., Hunnicutt, S., Klatt, D. and Pisoni, D. (1979) *Conversion of Unrestricted English Text to Speech*, MIT.

Atal, B. S. (1974) 'Effectiveness of Linear Prediction characteristics of the Speech Wave for Automatic Speaker Identification and Verification', *J. Acoust. Soc. Amer.*, **55**, 1304–1312.

Atal, B. S. (1976) 'Automatic Recognition of Speakers from their Voices', *IEEE*, **64**, (4), 460–475.

Atal, B. S. and Hanauer, S. L. (1971) 'Speech Synthesis and Synthesis by Linear Prediction of the Speech Wave', *J. Acoust. Soc. Amer.* **50**, 637-655.

Bahl, L. R., Jelineck, F. and Mercer, R. L. (1983) 'A Maximum Likelihood Approach to Continuous Speech Recognition', *IEEE Trans. on Pattern Analysis and Machine Intelligence*, **5**, (2), 179–190.

Baker, J. S. and Baker, J. K. (1983) 'Aspects of Stochastic Modelling for Speech Recognition', *Speech Technology*, **1**, (4).

Bell, D. A. (1968) *Information Theory and its Engineering Applications*, Pitman.

Biermann, A. W., Fineman, L. and Gilbert, K. C. (1985) 'An Imperative Sentence Processor for Voice Interactive Applications', *ACM Trans. Office Systems*, **3**, (4), 321–346.

Bristow, G. (1984) *Electronic Speech Synthesis: Techniques, Technology and Applications*, Granada.

Bruckert, E., Minow, M. and Tetschner, W. (1983) 'Three-Tiered Software and VLSI Aid Developmental System to Read Text Aloud', *Electronics*, **55**, (8), 133–138.

Campanella, S. J. (1976) 'Digital Speech Interpolation', *COMSAT Tech. Rev.*, **6**, 127–158.

Cappellini, V. (ed.) (1985) *Data Compression and Error Control Techniques with Applications*, Academic Press.

Cole, R. A. (1973) 'Listening for Mispronunciations: A Measure of What we Hear During Speech', *J. Perception and Psychophysics*, **13**, 153–156.

Cole, R. A., Stern, R. M. and Lasry, M. J. (1984) 'Performing Fine

Phonetic Distinctions: Templates vs Features', In *Symposium on Invariance and Variability of Speech Processors*, Erlbaum, Hillsdale N.J.

Delgutte, B. (1984) 'Speech Coding in the Auditory Nerve: Processing Schemes for Vowel-like Sounds', *J. Acoust. Soc. Amer.*, **75**, (3), 879-886.

De Mori, R. (1983) *Computer Models of Speech Using Fuzzy Algorithms*, Plenum Press.

De Mori, R., Lam, L. and Gilloux, M. (1987) 'Learning and Plan Refinement in a Knowledge-Based System for Automatic Speech Recognition', *IEEE Trans. Pattern Analysis and Machine Intelligence*, 289–305.

Derouault, A. and Merialdo, B. (1986) 'Natural Language Modelling for Phoneme-to-Text', *IEEE Trans. Pattern Analysis and Machine Intelligence*, **8**, (6), 742–749.

Dixon, N. R. and Martin, T. B. (1978) *Automatic Speech and Speaker Recognition*, IEEE Press, Selected Reprint Series.

Dixon, N. R. and Silverman, H. F. (1976) 'A General Language-Operated Decision Implementation System (GLODIS): Is Application to Continuous-Speech Segmentation', *IEEE Trans. Acoust., Speech, and Signal Processing*, **24**, (2), 137–162.

Dusek, L., Schalk, T. B. and McMahan, M. (1983) 'Voice Recognition Joins Speech on Programmable Board', *Electronics*, **55**, (8), 133–138.

Elovitz, H. S., Johnson, R., McHugh, A. and Shore, J. E. (1976) 'Letter-to-Sound Rules for Automatic Translation of English Text to Phonetics', *IEEE Trans. Acoust., Speech, and Signal Processing*, **24**, (6), 446–459.

Erman, L. D., Hayes-Roth, F., Lesser, V. R. and Reddy, D. (1980) 'The Hearsay II Speech Understanding System: Integrating Knowledge to Resolve Uncertainty', *Computing Surveys*, **12**, (2), 213–253.

Fallside, F. and Woods, W. A. (1985) *Computer Speech Processing*, Prentice-Hall.

Fujimura, O. (1975) 'Syllable as a Unit of Speech Recognition', *IEEE Trans. on Acoust.*, Speech, and Signal Processing, **23**, 82–87.

Fujimura, O., Macchi, M. J. and Lovins, J. B. (1977) 'Demisyllables and Affixes for Speech Synthesis', *Proc. 9th Int. Congr. on Acoust.*, 51–53.

Gordon, D. and Brown, A. (1987) 'Resolving Inconsistency: A Computational Model of Word Naming', *J. Memory and Languages*, 1–24.

Gray, A. H. Jr and Markel, J. D. (1975) 'A Normalised Digital Filter Structure', *IEEE Trans. Acoust., Speech, and Signal Processing*, **23**, 268–277.

Haton, J. P. (1982) *Automatic Speech Analysis and Recognition*, Reidel Publishing Co.

Hunt, M. J., Lenning, M. and Mermelstein, P. (1980) 'Experiments in Syllable Based Recognition of Continuous Speech', *Proc. IEEE Int. Conf. on Acoust., Speech, and Signal Processing*, Denver, CO, 880–883.

Huttenlocher, D. P. and Zue, V. W. (1983) 'Phonetic and Lexical Contraints in Speech Recognition', *AAAI Internat. Conf.*, Washington DC.

Huttenlocher, D. P. and Zue, V. W. (1984) 'A Model of Lexical Access from Partial Phonetic Information', *Proc. ICASSP-84, IEEE,* **26,** 26.4.1–26.4.4.

Jayant, N. S. and Noll, P. (1984) *Digital Coding of Waveforms: Principles and Applications to Speech and Video*, Prentice-Hall.

Jelineck, F. (1976) 'Continuous Speech Recognition by Statistical Methods', *Proc. IEEE,* **64,** 532–556.

Jelineck, F., Mercer, R. L. and Bahl, L. R. (1983) 'Continuous Speech Recognition: Statistical Methods', *IEEE Trans. Pattern Analysis and Machine Intelligence,* **5**.

Johnson, S. R., Connolly, J. H. and Edmonds, E. A. (1985) 'Spectrogram Analysis: A Knowledge-Based Approach to Automatic Speech Recognition', in *Research and Development in Expert Systems*, Bramer, M. A. (editor), Cambridge University Press, pp. 95–103.

Kewley-Port, D. (1983) 'Time-Varying Features as Correlates of Place of Articulation in Stop Consonants', *J. Acoust. Soc. Amer.,* **73**, 322–335.

Klatt, D. H. (1982) 'Speech Processing Strategies Based on Auditory Models', in *The Representation of Speech in the Peripheral Auditory System*, Carlson, R. and Granstrom, B. (editors), Elsevier/North-Holland, New York, pp. 181-196.

Ladefoged, P. (1966) *Elements of Acoustic Phonetics*, Oliver & Boyd.

Lea, W. A. (1980) *Trends in Speech Recognition*, Prentice-Hall.

Lee, D. L. & Lochovsky, F. H. (1983) 'Voice response systems', *Computing Surveys,* **15,** (4), 351–374.

Levinson, S. E. (1984) 'A Unified Theory of Composite Pattern Analysis for Automatic Speech Recognition', in *Computer Speech Processing*, Fallside, F. and Woods, W. (editors), Prentice-Hall.

Lowerre, B. T. (1977) 'Dynamic Speaker Adaptation in the HARPY Speech Recognition System', *IEEE Trans. Acoust., Speech, and Signal Processing*, 788–790.

Makhoul, J. (1975) 'Linear Prediction: A Tutorial Review', *Proc. IEEE,* **63,** 561–580.

Makhoul, J. (1977) 'Stable and Efficient Lattice Methods for Linear Prediction', *IEEE Trans. Acoust., Speech, and Signal Processing,* **25,** 423–428.

Makhoul, J. (1978) 'A Class of All-Zero Lattice Digital Filters Properties and Applications', *IEEE Trans. Acoust., Speech, and Signal Processing,* **26,** 304–314.

Miller, J. L. (1981) 'Effect of Speaking Rate on Segmental Distinction', in *Perspective on the Study of Speech,* Eimas, P. D. and Miller, J. L. (editors), Erlbaum, Hillsdale, NJ.

Morton, J. (1964) 'The Effects of Context on the Visual Duration Threshold for Words', *Br. J. Psychol.* **55,** 165–180.

Myers, C. S. and Levinson, S. E. (1982) 'Speaker Independent Connected

Word Recognition Using a Syntax Directed Dynamic Programming Procedure', *IEEE Trans. Acoust., Speech, and Signal Processing,* **30,** 561–565.

Neff, R. (1982) 'Japanese Welcome Voice Recognition', *Electronics,* **55,** (3), 97–98.

Neff, R. (1983) 'Machine Translation Regains Its Voice', *Electronics,* **56,** (4), 82–83.

Nooteboom, S. G. (1981) 'Speech Rate and Segmental Perception for the Role of Words in Phoneme Identification', in *The Cognitive Representation of Speech,* Myers, T., Laver J. and Anderson, J. (editors), North Holland.

Nuggehally, S. J. (1974) 'Digital Coding of Speech Waveforms PCM, DPCM, and DM Quantisers', *Proc. IEEE,* **62,** 611–632.

O'Connor, J. D. (1984) *Phonetics: A Simple and Practical Introduction to the Nature and Use of Sound in Language,* Penguin.

O'Shaughnessy, D. (1983) 'Automatic Speech Synthesis', *IEEE Commun.* **21,** (9), 26–34.

Rabiner, L. R. and Levinson, S. E. (1981) 'Isolated and Connected Word Recognition—Theory and selected applications', *IEEE Trans. Commun.,* **29,** 621–659.

Rabiner, L. R. and Schafer, R. W. (1978) *Digital Processing of Speech Signals,* Prentice-Hall, Englewood Cliffs.

Radhakrishnan, T. and Castillo, R. (1981) 'Speech Synthesis from Text Based on Syllables', *Conf. CMCCS/ACCHO,* 223–231.

Reddy, D. R. (1975) *Speech Recognition: Invited Papers of the IEEE Symposium,* Academic Press.

Rosenberg, A. E. (1973) 'Listener Performance in Speaker Identification Task', *IEEE Trans. Audio. Electroacoust.,* **21,** 221–225.

Rosenberg, A. E., Rabiner, L. R., Wilpon, J. G. and Kahn, D. (1983) 'Demisyllable-Based Isolated Word Recognition Systems', *IEEE Trans. Acoust., Speech, and Signal Processing,* **31,** (3), 713–726.

Ruske, G. and Schotola, T. (1978) 'An Approach to Speech Recognition Using Syllable Decision Units', *Proc. IEEE Int. Conf. on Acoust., Speech, and Signal Processing,* Tulsa, OK, pp. 722–725.

Sakoe, H. and Chiba, S. (1978) 'Dynamic Programming Algorithm Optimisation for Spoken Word Recognition', *IEEE Trans. Acoust. Speech, and Signal Processing,* **26,** (1), 43–49.

Samuel, A. G. (1987) 'Lexical Uniqueness Effects on Phonemic Restoration', *J. Memory and Languages,* 36–56.

Schwartz, R., Chow, Y., Roucos, S., Krasner, M. and Makhoul, J. (1984) 'Improved Hidden Markov Modelling of Phonemes for Continuous Speech Recognition', *Proc. IEEE Int. Conf. on Acoustic Speech and Signal Processing,* San Diego, CA.

Shannon, C. E. (1948) 'A Mathematical Theory of Communication', *Bell Sys. Tech. J.,* **27,** (July), pp. 379–423, (October), 623–656.

Shannon, C. E. and Weaver, W. (1949) 'The mathematical Theory of

Communication', University of Illinois Press.

Shipman, D. W. and Zue, V. W. (1982) 'Properties of Large Lexicons: Implications for Advanced Isolated Word Recognition Systems', *Proc.*, ICASSP–82, 546–549.

Simon, J. C. (1980) *Spoken Language Generation and Understanding*, Reidel Publishing Co.

Singh, S. and Singh, K. S. (1976) *Phonetics: Principles and Practices*, University Park Press.

Srulovicz, P. and Goldstein, J. L. (1983) 'A Central Spectrum Model: A Synthesis of Auditory-Nerve Timing and Place Cues in Monaural Communication of Frequency Spectrum', *J. Acoust. Soc. Amer.*, **73**, (4), 1266–1276.

Tulving, E. and Gold, C. (1963) 'Stimulus Information and Contextual Information as Determinants of Tachistoscopic Recognition of Words', *J. of Exp. Psychol.*, **66**, 319–327.

Vaissiere, J. (1985) 'Speech Recognition: A Tutorial', in *Computer Speech Processing*, Fallside, F. and Woods, W. A. (editors), Prentice-Hall, pp. 191–236.

Waibel, A. (1982) 'Very Large Vocabulary Recognition, Using Prosodic and Spectral Filters', *J. Acoust. Soc. Amer.*, **72**.

Yannakoudakis, E. J. (1983) 'Expert Spelling Error Analysis and Correction', *Proceedings, 7th ASLIB Conference on Informatics*, University of Cambridge, pp. 39–52.

Yannakoudakis, E. J. (1985) 'Voice I/O: Problems and Perspectives', *Computer Bulletin, Series III*, **1**, (3), 10–12.

Zue, V. W. (1985) 'The Use of Speech Knowledge in Automatic Speech Recognition', *Proc.*, *IEEE*, **73**, (11), 1602–1615.

Zue, V. W. and Cole, R. A. (1979) 'Experiments on Spectrogram Reading', *Proc. IEEE Int. Conf. on Acoustic speech and Signal Processing*, pp. 116–119.

Index

ELLIS HORWOOD BOOKS IN COMPUTING SCIENCE
General Editors: Professor JOHN CAMPBELL, University College London, and BRIAN L. MEEK, King's College London (KQC), University of London

Series in Computers and Their Applications
Series Editor: BRIAN L. MEEK, Computer Centre, King's College London (KQC), University of London

Computer Communitcations and Networking